MANAGEMENT ACCOUNTS

Management accounts

How to use them to control your business

Tony Skone

Gower

Published by
Gower Publishing Limited
Gower House
Croft Road
Aldershot
Hampshire GU11 3HR
England

Gower
Old Post Road
Brookfield
Vermont 05036
USA

Tony Skone has asserted his right under the Copyright, Designs and Patents Act 1988 to be identified as the author of this work.

British Library Cataloguing in Publication Data

Skone, Tony
  Management Accounts: How to Use Them to Control Your Business
  I. Title
  658.1511

ISBN 0–566–07483–4

Library of Congress Cataloging-in-Publication Data

Skone, Tony, 1939–
    Management accounts: how to use them to control your business / Tony Skone.
      p.   cm.
    Includes index.
    ISBN 0–566–07483–4
    1. Managerial accounting.   2. Financial statements.   I. Title.
  HF5657.4.S54   1995
  858.15'11—dc20

94–42507
CIP

Typeset in Palatino and Helvetica by Poole Typesetting (Wessex) Ltd and printed in Great Britain at the University Press, Cambridge.

Contents

List of tables

List of figures

Introduction

Since 1974 I have participated in the running of courses such as 'Finance for the Non-Financial Manager', 'Management Accounting for the Non-Accountant' and 'Understanding Company Accounts'. One advantage of this protracted spell of lecturing has been to appreciate what it is that **managers** want to achieve.

What are managers expecting to get out of the course that they cannot get from their own accountants? The answer, nine times out of ten, is 'to understand the jargon'. (One delegate, when asked what he most wanted out of the course, answered 'myself'.) The majority response highlights the overriding problem in this area: the classic non-communicator (the accountant) attempting to communicate with the classic financial illiterate (the manager).

All too often, the accountant is seen as someone who spends half the year doing the budgets and the other half doing the annual accounts. The manager, on the receipt of financial information, adopts the ostrich pose and feigns understanding by either nodding at the appropriate times or gazing into the distance.

What accountants have to do is become better communicators while managers have to become financially literate, that is, they have to learn to speak the language of business – **money**.

The story that best illustrates this non-meeting of minds concerns Richard Branson and a fellow director of Virgin who lose their way in a hot air balloon. They eventually hover over an isolated farmhouse and shout down, 'Is anybody there?'

Eventually a man opens the front door in his pyjamas, looks up and says, 'What can I do for you?'

Branson calls down, 'Can you tell us where we are, please?'

The man on the ground answers, 'You're in a hot air balloon 50 feet above my house.'

At that moment a gust of air blows the balloon away and Branson turns to his fellow director and says, 'Just our luck, the only person for miles around had to be a chartered accountant.'

'How did you know that?' his colleague asks.

'Because what he told us was one hundred per cent accurate and one hundred per cent bloody useless!'

The story does not end there, however. When the accountant goes back into his house his wife asks him, 'Who were you talking to?'

'Oh, just two directors', he replies.

'How did you know they were two directors?' she asks.

'Because they were full of hot air, had no idea where they were and no idea where they were going.'

Management accounting has been defined as the provision of financial information to managers to help them in the key areas of:

- planning
- controlling
- decision making.

Management accounting has also been described as 'attention directing'. In particular, managers need to know when things are not going according to plan, rather than be told things they already know or already expect. Management's time is limited. It is impossible to control everything, so the management accounting system should highlight those areas where remedial action needs to be taken.

The three cardinal rules of financial reporting are:

1 form
2 frequency
3 accuracy.

1   Form

The form of the information should be such that it is intelligible to the recipient. No prior knowledge should be assumed by the providers of this information.

In some instances it might be better to substitute units for £s. For example, the supervisor of a machine shop should be able to take some action on being informed that in month 3 his section used 400 kilos of copper compared to an expected usage of 350 kilos. Being informed that there was an adverse material usage variance of £900 and a favourable price variance of £350 might not mean much to him.

2   Frequency

How frequently should financial information be provided? The answer should be 'as and when needed'. Most management accounting information is supplied monthly but some might more appropriately be supplied quarterly or even annually, whilst other information such as sales, bank balance, cash receipts and so on might be supplied weekly.

3   Accuracy

How accurate should the information be? Although we might expect that such information is 100 per cent correct this is not always true. Ensuring 100 per cent accuracy takes time and costs money. It might be better to get 90 per cent accurate information soon after the event rather than 100 per cent accurate information six months later. To tell a foreman in December that the labour cost for job 123 completed in June was £2000 more than planned is unlikely to generate remedial action.

It is also important to ensure that the cost of providing such general financial information does not exceed the benefit obtained.

1 The movement of money in a business

This chapter will explain where money comes from and where it goes to in a business. The primary financial statements – the profit and loss statement, the balance sheet and the cash flow forecast – will be introduced together with such concepts as **gearing, working capital** and **depreciation**. We will track the progress of a newly established company, Timberland Ltd.

The money put into the business, the capital, could be invested in a non-risk situation such as a bank deposit account or building society to generate a return of X per cent p.a. In the long term the return on the capital employed in the business must therefore exceed X per cent to compensate the investors for the risk they have taken. The risk associated with such an investment is twofold:

1 that there is no return (profit) on the investment;
2 that all the investment is lost, that is, the company goes into liquidation.

Risk and return

When considering an investment, whether in property, antiques, commodities or a business, there are two basic questions an investor must ask:

1 What is the likely return on the investment?
2 What is the risk of losing all the money invested?

In a business situation the answer to the first question is provided by the **profit and loss statement.** This shows what the return has been in the past. Studying such statements covering a number of years will enable an

5

investor to establish the trends which will indicate what return might reasonably be expected in the future.

The answer to the second question is indicated by the **balance sheet**. The balance sheet is a listing of the assets and liabilities of a company on a given date. It shows where a business has put its money and where that money came from. It is sometimes known as a 'where to and where from' statement.

The risks are greater if the short-term liabilities are more than the short-term assets and if the capital provided by lenders is more than that provided by shareholders.

If short-term capital is more than long-term capital then the risks are again greater. Another indication of higher risk would be when short-term capital has been used to finance long-term assets.

The third primary statement of business progress is the **cash flow forecast** which shows where the money will be coming from in the future and where it will be going to. It is a forecast of what the bank balance is expected to be at the end of each month. It will show projected cash balances or projected overdrafts. It is also called the **cash budget**.

The business plan

Before a business is set up the owners should produce a business plan, the purpose of which is to ascertain whether the project is a viable proposition. The initial business plan will disclose:

- what the company plans to sell
- how much the products will cost to produce
- how much the product will be sold for
- the size of the market
- who and where the customers are
- who and where the competition is
- what money must be spent on – for example, premises, equipment, motor vehicles, people, advertising and (most important of all!) accountants
- how much money is needed to start
- where the money will come from
- who the shareholders and senior managers will be
- the number of employees
- business strategy – the five year plan
- shorter-term objectives – the twelve month budgets.

Timberland Ltd is established to make and sell furniture. The business plan indicates an initial capital requirement of £100 000. Where is this to come from?

As shown in Figure 1.1, the only two sources are:

1 the owners (shareholders) who provide share capital and
2 the lenders who provide loan capital.

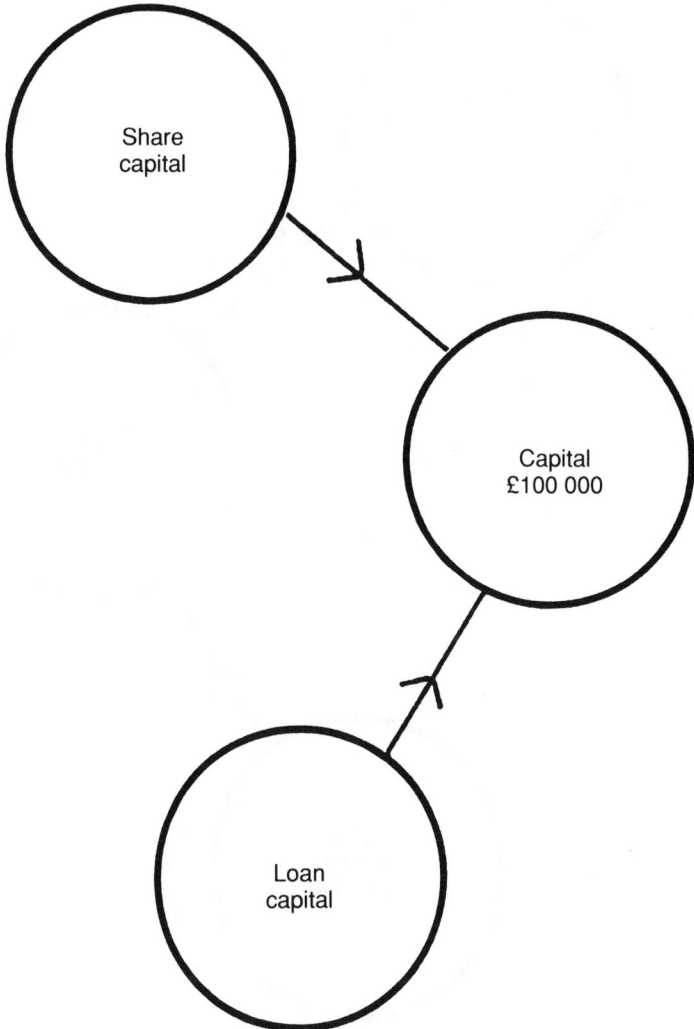

Figure 1.1   Sources of capital

How much of the £100 000 should come from shareholders and how much from lenders? The deciding factor is how much the shareholders have to invest. If the shareholders have £70 000 to invest, the loan capital would need to be £30 000. To get a loan of £30 000 the bank would need to be convinced that the company:

- could pay the interest
- could repay the loan
- had security of more than £30 000
- knew what it was doing.

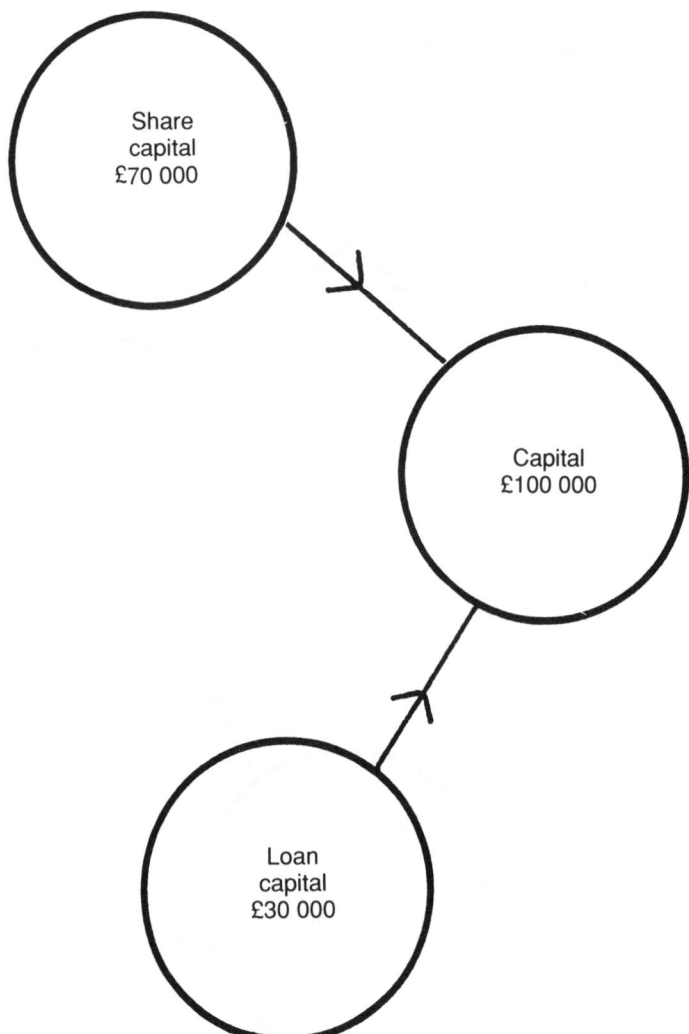

Figure 1.2   Relative amounts of share capital and loan capital

The bank would want to see the business plan and would use the information contained in it to answer the above points.

The situation now is seen in Figure 1.2. The relative amounts of loan capital and shareholders' capital is expressed in the **gearing** or **leverage**. In this company the gearing is expressed as 42 per cent, that is the loan is 42 per cent of the shareholders' funds $\left(\dfrac{30}{70} \times 100\%\right)$.

The next question to be considered is how much money the company would have in the bank on day 1. If the shareholders have put £70 000 into the business and the lenders £30 000, then the opening cash balance must be £100 000 (see Figure 1.3).

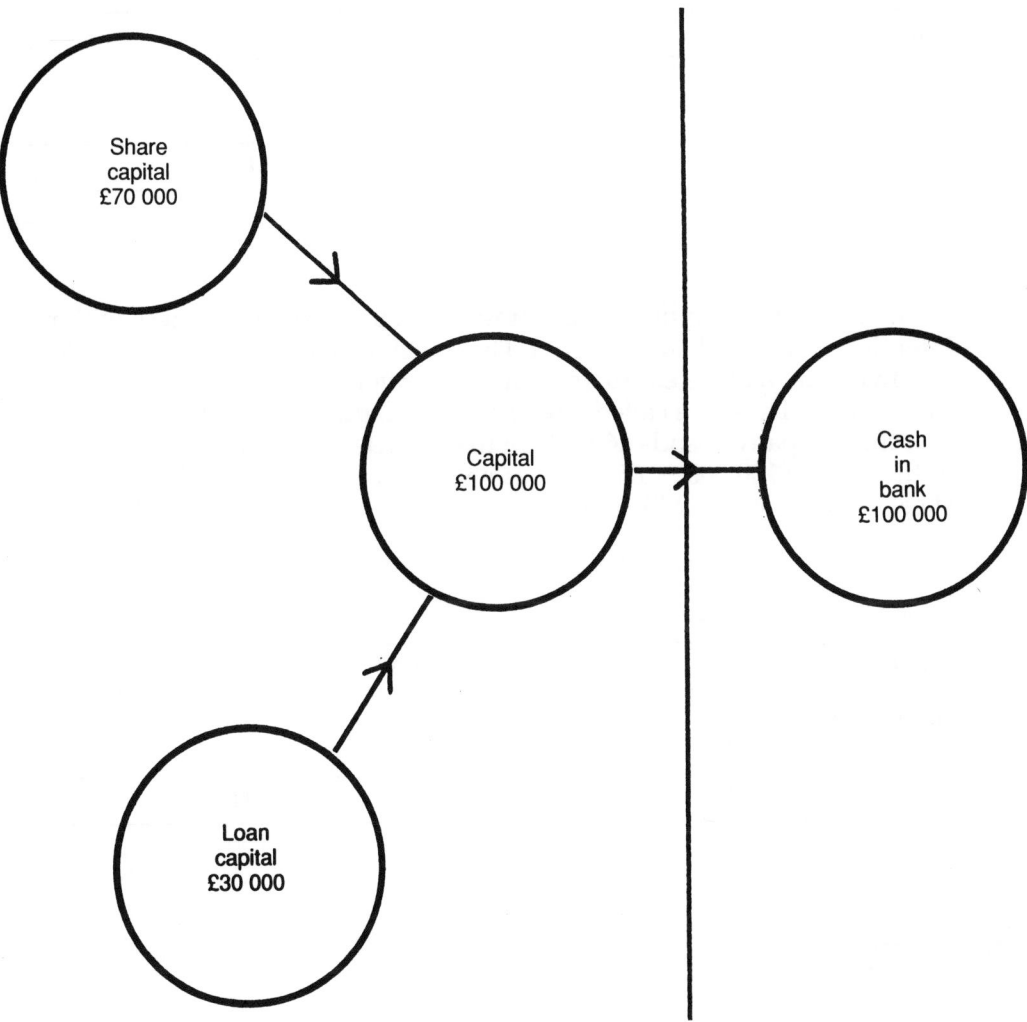

Figure 1.3   Cash in bank as at day 1

Assets and liabilities

A statement can now be drawn up showing what the business owns (assets) and what the business owes (liabilities), as in Table 1.1.

The only asset the business has is £100 000 in the bank. The liabilities are share capital (owed by the company to the shareholders) of £70 000 and loan capital (owed by the company to the lender) of £30 000.

The assets and liabilities equal one another – **they balance!** The statement in Table 1.1 is called a **balance sheet** – and is probably the simplest balance sheet you will see.

Table 1.1   A picture of the liabilities and assets of Timberland Ltd as at day 1

Liabilities (£000s)		Assets (£000s)	
Share capital	70	Cash in bank	100
Loan capital	30		
	100		100

The company then purchases things to be used in the business with no intention of selling them at a profit. These include land and buildings, plant and machinery, office equipment and motor vehicles. It spends £60 000 on these assets. These are called **fixed assets** or **capital expenditure**.

If the company spends £60 000 on fixed assets it would have £40 000 left in the bank (£100 000 − £60 000), as shown in Figure 1.4, and the balance sheet would now look like this.

Table 1.2   Balance sheet as at day 2

Liabilities (£000s)		Assets (£000s)	
Share capital	70	Cash in bank	40
Loan capital	30	Fixed assets	60
	100		100

Calculating profit

Timberland Ltd then buys things to produce profits. These are as follows:

Materials (timber etc.)	£20 000
Labour	£10 000
Overheads	£10 000
Total	£40 000

The £40 000 expenditure on things to sell at a profit is called **revenue expenditure**. If these things were purchased with cash, the bank balance would now be nil (see Figure 1.5).

Timberland also buys some materials on credit. These cost £10 000. This means that material purchases amount to £30 000 in total and that the company has creditors of £10 000 (assuming they haven't paid anything to their suppliers).

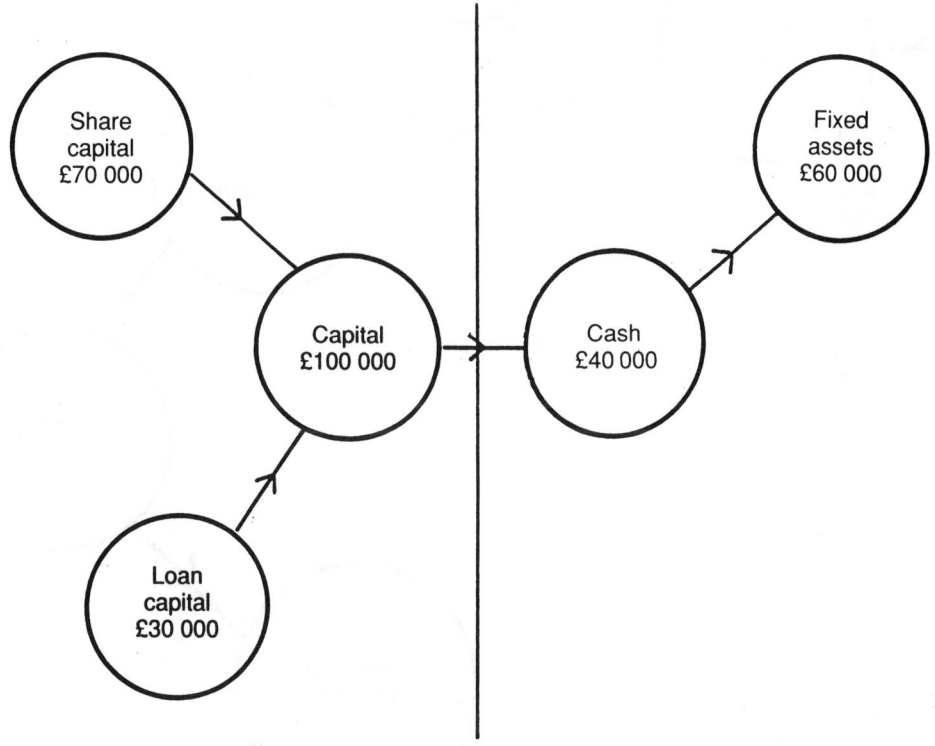

Figure 1.4   Cash in bank as at day 2

Before calculating the profit (if any) certain things have to be ascertained:

- How much depreciation to charge on the fixed assets to reflect the loss of value in the first year. If the £60 000 fixed assets are estimated to last five years, the depreciation each year could be taken as £60000 divided by 5 = £12 000.
- Are any invoices of expenses yet to arrive? It is estimated that the interest bill for the final quarter, the telephone bill and the gas and electricity will amount to £4000. These are called **accrued expenses,** or **accruals.**

The following are the revenue expenses for year 1:

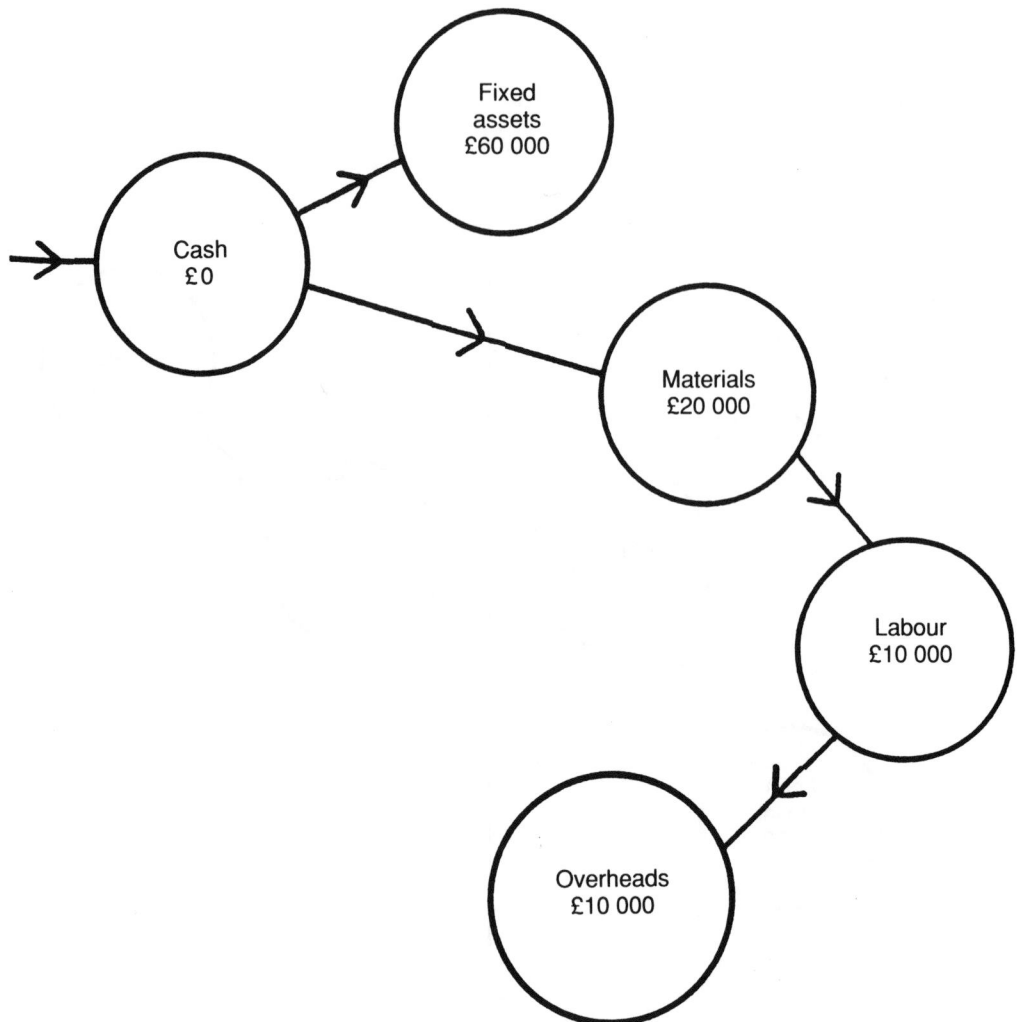

Figure 1.5   Capital and revenue expenditure

Materials	£30 000 (20 000 cash + 10 000 credit)
Labour	£10 000
Overheads	£10 000
Depreciation	£12 000 (note – no cash spent)
Accruals	£4 000
Total revenue expenses	£66 000

- The last question before calculating the profit is how much of the £66 000 is represented by stocks at the year end. The stock-take at the year end of raw materials, work in progress and finished goods gives a figure of £20 000 (at cost). The cost of the goods **sold** was therefore:

Total revenue expenses	£66 000 (see above)
Less cost of stock	£20 000
Cost of goods sold	£46 000

To work out the profit, all the invoices sent out to customers in year 1 must be added together. This gives the sales or revenue (or turnover) figure.

If the sales figure was £80 000 and the company has received £10 000 of this £80 000 from its customers, the debtors at the year end must be:

Sales (invoices)	£80 000
Less receipts	£10 000
Debtors at year end	£70 000

The net profit before tax of Timberland Ltd is £34 000 (see Table 1.3). Some of the profit has to be appropriated to the Inland Revenue as corporation tax. Here the figure is £10 000. The net profit after tax, also known as the **earnings**, belongs to the shareholders. The directors of the company will decide how much, if any, of the earnings should be paid as dividends to the shareholders. The directors decide in this case to pay out 50 per cent of the earnings as dividends.

Table 1.3   Profit and loss account for year ended, Timberland Ltd

Sales	£80 000 (invoices)
Less cost of goods sold	£46 000
Net profit before tax	£34 000
Less tax	£10 000
Net profit after tax	£24 000
Less dividends	£12 000
Retained profit	£12 000

Notes:
- The tax has been estimated at £10 000 but is not yet due for payment.
- The dividends have been declared but have not yet been paid.
- The retained profit forms the third source of long-term capital. Retained profits since the start of a business are also called **reserves**.

The balance sheet

Table 1.4 on page 14 shows the balance sheet of Timberland Ltd at the end of year 1. It provides a listing of the assets and liabilities of the business *on that date*.

Table 1.4 Balance sheet as at year end, Timberland Ltd

Liabilities (£000s)			Assets (£000s)		
Share capital		70	Fixed assets (cost less deprn.)		48
Reserves		12	*Current assets*		
Shareholders' funds		82	Stocks	20	
Loan capital		30	Debtors	70	
			Cash	10	
					100
Current liabilities					
Creditors	10				
Accruals	4				
Corporation tax	10				
Proposed dividends	12				
		36			
Total		148	Total		148

The fixed assets have to be shown as follows:

Cost	Less depreciation to date	Net book value
£60 000	£12 000	£48 000

The assets to be turned into cash in the next year are called **current assets**. These are listed as follows:

Stocks at year end (at cost)	£20 000
Debtors	£70 000
Cash	£10 000
	£100 000

The long-term liabilities, as before, are the **share capital** and the **loan capital**. Another long-term liability is the profit owed to the shareholders by the business, the reserves of £12 000 (retained profit for year 1).

The short-term, or current, liabilities are as follows:

Creditors	£10 000
Accruals	£4 000
Corporation tax	£10 000
Proposed dividends	£12 000
	£36 000

The more usual approach to balance sheets today is to re-organise some of the figures in Table 1.4. The current assets and current liabilities are netted

Table 1.5   Balance sheet as at year end, Timberland Ltd (in £000s)

Fixed assets at cost			60
Less depreciation			12
Net book value (NBV)			48
Current assets			
Stocks		20	
Debtors		70	
Cash		10	
		100	
Less current liabilities			
Creditors	10		
Accruals	4		
Corporation tax	10		
Proposed dividends	12		
		36	
Net current assets			64
Total assets less current liabilities			112
Less long-term loans			30
Net assets			82
Financed by:			
Share capital			70
Reserves			12
Shareholders' funds			82

Notes: The difference between current assets and current liabilities is called **net current assets** (£64 000). It is also known as **working capital**.

off on the assets side. The left and right presentation has been dropped and a vertical layout is now used (see Table 1.5).

Figure 1.6 shows that the year-end cash balance is £10 000. A cash flow summary for year 1 would be useful to show how this balance was arrived at. A similar layout, month by month, will be used to produce the cash flow forecast (see Table 1.6).

Summary of key points relating to the business model

1 Depreciation must be included as part of the expenses but it does not affect cash flow as it is not paid out in cash.
2 The accruals must be included as part of the expenses for the year but do not affect the cash flow until paid.
3 The net profit will, at the year end, be subject to tax and perhaps partly appropriated to the shareholders as dividends.

   • The profits retained in the business are known as **reserves** and are a further liability to the shareholders (it is their profits that are being retained by the business). It must be emphasised that reserves are not necessarily the same as money in the bank. The profits retained

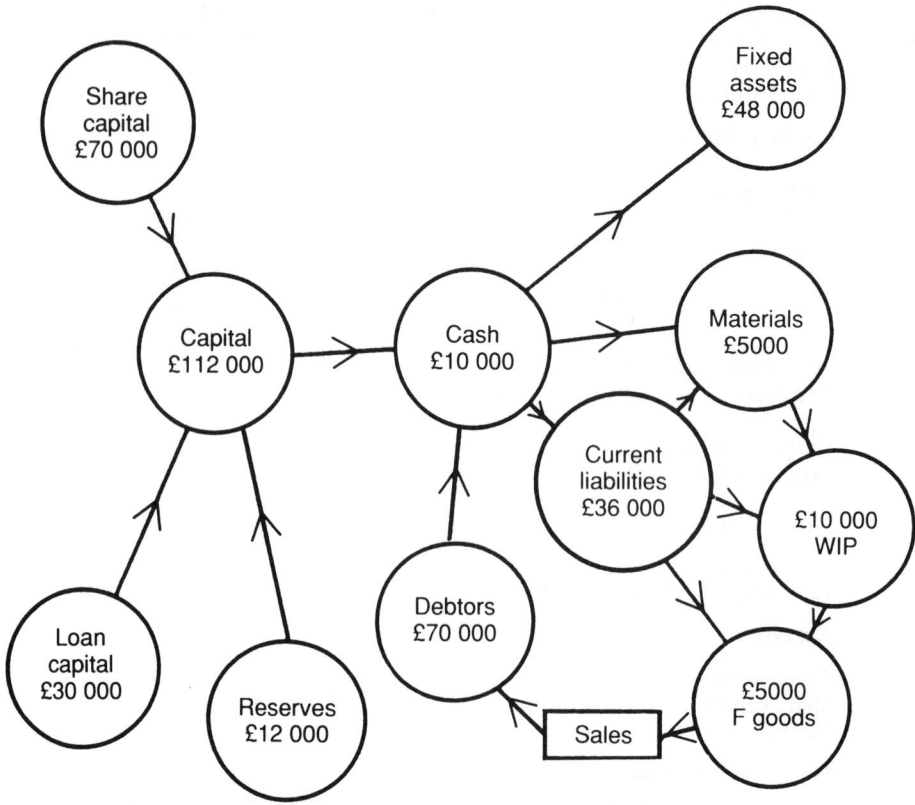

Figure 1.6   End of year model

Note that the reserves (retained profits) do not necessarily equal the money in the bank. Reserves are profits owed to the shareholders which have been used to make the business *grow.* The closing stock is made up of £5000 of materials, £10 000 of work in progress and £5000 of finished goods.

Table 1.6   Cash flow for year 1

Receipts	
Share capital	70
Loan capital	30
Debtor receipts	10
Total receipts	110
Payments	
Fixed assets	60
Materials	20
Labour	10
Overheads	10
Total payments	100
Surplus/(deficit)	10
Opening balance	0
Closing balance	10

Note: Depreciation, which is an expense in the profit and loss account, *never* appears as a payment on the cash flow.

will be used to finance fixed assets and current assets. They are used to make the business grow.

- The total of the share capital and the reserves is called the **shareholders' funds** (also known as **equity**). It is also called net worth.

How did the company perform?

Certain figures can be calculated to see whether it has all been worthwhile. These can be compared with previous years' figures (once the company has got going), with competitors' figures, with the average for the industry and with target figures.

Return on capital employed

This shows how the profit generated compares with the capital invested. The formula is:

$$\frac{profit}{capital} \times 100\%$$

$$= \frac{34}{112} \times 100\% = 30.4\%$$

Note: The 'profit' figure is the net profit before tax. The 'capital' figure is the total of the fixed assets and working capital.

Summary: An excellent result. Much higher than interest rates and higher return than would be obtained from a Building Society. Much better than the UK average.

Return on sales

This shows how much profit is being made as a percentage of sales. The formula is:

$$\frac{profit}{sales} \times 100\%$$

$$= \frac{34}{80} \times 100\% = 42.5\%$$

Note: The 'profit' figure is again the net profit before tax.

Summary: Much depends on trends and other similar companies' performance.

Liquidity

This shows whether the company can pay its short-term debts. The formula is:

current assets : current liabilities
= 100:36
= 2.78:1

Summary: No problems here. More than enough money in the till or coming into the till to pay the bills.

Debtor days

This shows the credit control performance. The formula is:

$$\frac{debtors}{sales} \times 365$$

$$= \frac{70}{80} \times 365$$

$$= 319 \text{ days}$$

Summary: Credit control looks non-existent in this company. However, sales may have been slow to build up and could have been made near the year end. It would be dangerous to read too much into the figures for a new company.

Working capital as percentage of sales

This shows how much 'luggage' the company has to carry to support its sales. The formula is:

$$\frac{working\ capital}{sales} \times 100\%$$

$$= \frac{64}{80} \times 100\%$$

$$= 80\%$$

Note: Working capital is the difference between current assets and current liabilities.

Summary: Future years will show whether this figure is reduced or increased. Companies should try to reduce the 'luggage' carried to support their sales.

Gearing

This shows how the borrowed capital compares to invested capital. The formula is:

$$\frac{\text{loan capital}}{\text{shareholders' funds}} \times 100\%$$

$$= \frac{30}{80} \times 100\%$$

$$= 36.6\%$$

Summary: The gearing has reduced because of the plough-back of profit into the business.

Summary of key financial statements

Table 1.7   The key financial statements

	The 3 Rs	Time period
Profit and loss	Return	Past
Balance sheet	Risk	Present
Cash flow forecast	'Readies'	Future

From the profit and loss statement are derived the techniques of costing and management accounting. From the balance sheet are derived the techniques of working capital control and analysis as well as project appraisal. The cash flow forecast or cash budget is the most important budget of all. It demonstrates a company's ability to fulfil its plans.

2 The development of management accounting

This chapter considers the development of management accounting from the basic financial accounting statements – the profit and loss statement and the balance sheet. It introduces the concept of cost classification, splitting costs into direct and indirect, fixed and variable.

The managers of Timberland Ltd would find that they could track the progress of the business by producing *monthly* statements of cash flow, profit and loss and a balance sheet. They could calculate certain ratios each month such as those shown on pages 17, 18 and 19.

Other useful additions to the system might include:

1 comparison between this month and the previous month
2 comparison between this month's actual figures and planned figures
3 results for the year to date – actual and planned
4 analysis of the sales, costs and profit over the different products.

Cost classification

To enable the above information to be produced, it is necessary to split costs up in various ways. This splitting, or classification, of costs can be achieved by breaking costs down into:

- direct and indirect costs
- fixed and variable costs
- controllable and uncontrollable costs.

Costs can be classified as in Figure 2.1.

Direct and indirect costs

If a cost can be directly identified to a product then it is a direct cost of that product. A cost directly related to a department is a direct cost of that

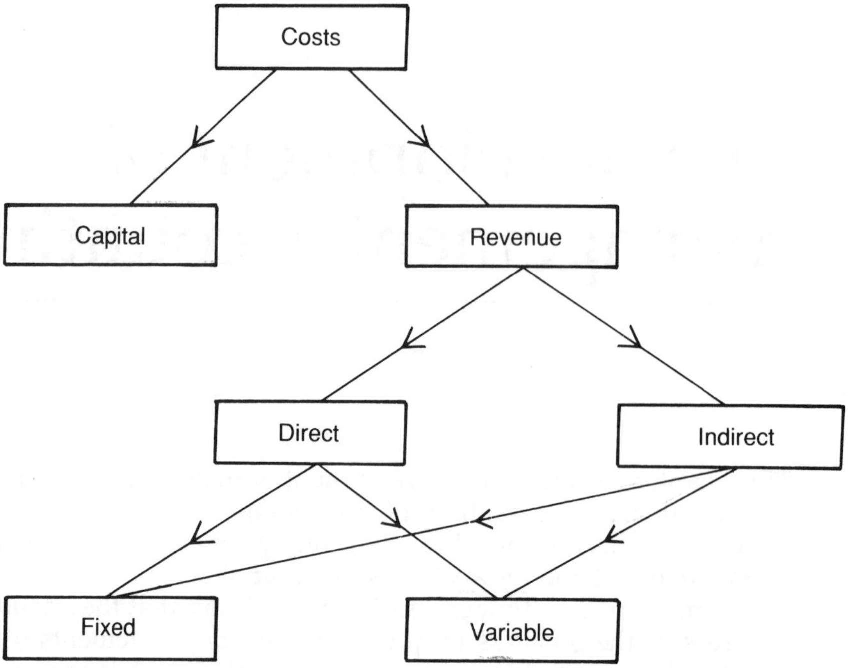

Figure 2.1   The classification of costs

department. Indirect costs are those that cannot be directly linked with a product or department.

A cost can be directly related to a department but be an indirect cost of a product. The salary of the machine shop supervisor would be a direct cost of the machine shop but an indirect cost of one of the many products manufactured in that department. For a service company, variable costs would include those costs directly related to the provision of the service, such as design, materials, travel or, perhaps, commission.

Fixed and variable costs

A cost that varies with activity is said to be variable. A cost that tends to remain at the same level irrespective of the level of activity is said to be fixed.

Examples of variable costs include:

- materials
- labour
- power
- commissions
- freight
- delivery
- royalties.

Examples of fixed costs include:

- rent
- rates
- heat and light
- salaries
- depreciation
- interest
- insurance.

Most direct costs tend to be variable whilst most indirect costs tend to be fixed. A direct cost is a cost that management has control over whilst an indirect cost is one that management does not have full control over.

Fixed and variable costs may be presented graphically as in Figure 2.2.

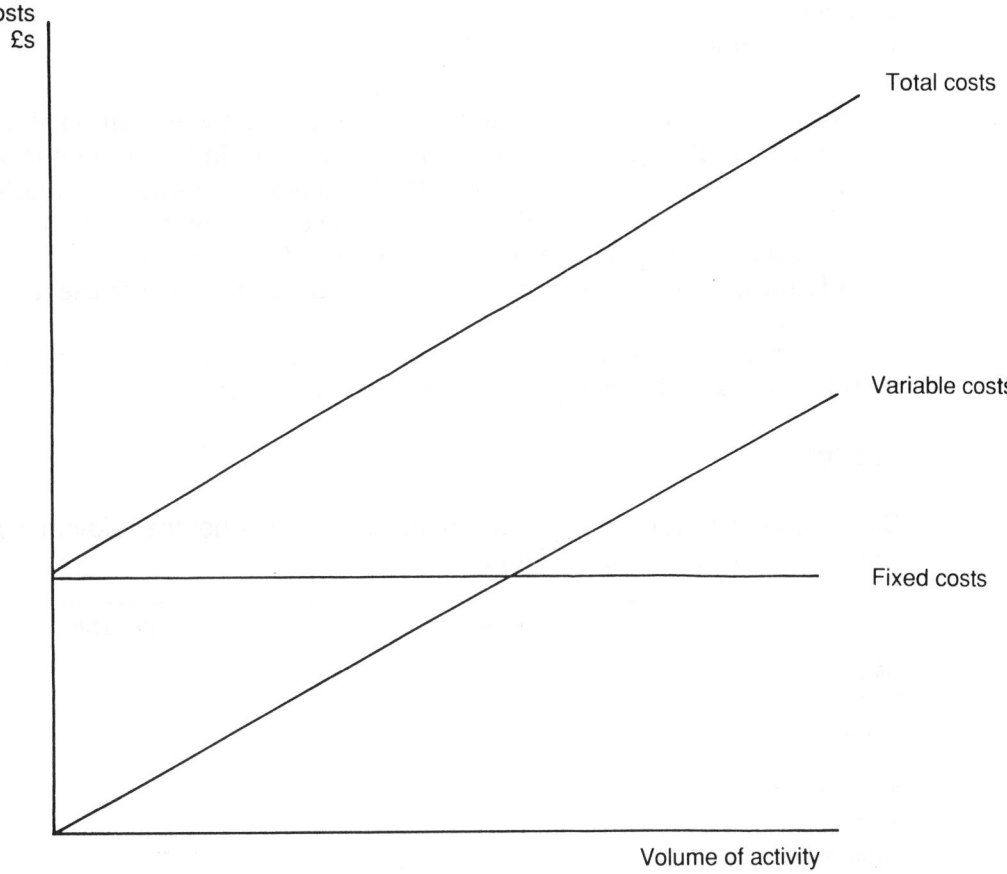

Figure 2.2   Fixed and variable costs

Controllable and uncontrollable costs

Controllable costs are those that can be influenced and changed by the actions of individual managers during a given time span. Uncontrollable costs are those that cannot be influenced by the action of individual managers during a given time period.

Examples of controllable costs are:

- materials
- labour
- power
- overtime
- telephone.

Examples of uncontrollable costs are:

- rent
- rates
- interest
- depreciation.

It should be noted that costs do not always fit exactly into one category or another. What might be fixed in one company could be variable in another. Direct labour might be paid on the basis of time in one organisation (fixed) and on the basis of output achieved in another (variable). Advertising of one specific product would be a direct cost of that product but advertising the company itself would be an indirect cost of the different products.

The format of a company's management accounts, as well as any cost classification, should be appropriate for that particular company.

EXERCISE

State, by putting a tick in the appropriate column, whether the relevant cost would tend to be fixed or variable.

	Fixed	Variable
Rent		
Rates		
Power		
Direct materials		
Advertising		
Interest		
Depreciation		
Direct labour		
Heat and light		
Salaries		
Royalties		
Sales commission		
Repairs		
Maintenance		

ANSWER

	Fixed	Variable
Rent	*	
Rates	*	
Telephone	*	
Power		*
Direct materials		*
Advertising	*	
Interest	*	
Depreciation	*	
Direct labour		*
Heat and light	*	
Salaries	*	
Royalties		*
Sales commission		*
Repairs		*
Maintenance	*	

You may not agree with all the above answers. Many costs display both fixed and variable tendencies and what is fixed in one business may be variable in another. Many costs are semi-variable in that they vary with activity but not directly, for example, repairs, maintenance, electricity and direct labour.

Advertising expenditure is a fixed cost because the advertising budget is normally fixed at the beginning of the year. It may be cut back if business is better than expected or increased if business is bad. However, it does not in the short term tend to vary with activity.

EXERCISE

Mark the following with a C (controllable) or U (uncontrollable) to illustrate your understanding of this cost classification. The costs relate to an assembly department in a factory.

- Direct labour
- Direct materials
- Overtime
- Power
- Rent and rates
- Heat and light
- Central head office charges.

ANSWER

Direct labour is partly controllable by the manager of this department in that the manager would have some control over the efficiency of the labour force. The number of people employed and their hourly rates would not be under this manager's control.

The direct material cost would again be partly under the control of the cost centre manager in so far as efficiency in the use of the material was concerned. The prices paid for the materials would be the responsibility of the purchasing manager.

Overtime may be the result of idle time or re-working of materials in which case it would be controllable. If it was the result of unexpected demand it would be largely uncontrollable.

Power would be partly controllable as far as efficiency was concerned but uncontrollable with regard to its unit cost.

The remaining costs would be uncontrollable by the individual manager (although the manager may have some control over heat and light in the department).

Classification of profit

Gross profit

The difference between sales and direct costs is known as **gross profit**. Alternative expressions include **gross margin** and **contribution**. For example:

Sales	£100 000
Less direct costs	£80 000
Gross profit	£20 000

The gross profit as a percentage of sales is 20 per cent and this is an important figure in the calculation of break-even (see page 44).

Many companies arrive at their selling price by adding a **mark-up** to direct cost. In the above example the mark-up would be expressed as 25 per cent (20/80 x 100).

Trading or operating profit

This is the profit from the day-to-day operating of the business, the profit generated from the core activities. It is the difference between the gross profit and the indirect expenses. For example:

Sales		£100 000
Less direct costs		£80 000
Gross profit		£20 000
Less indirect expenses:		
Production	£10 000	
Administration	£3 000	
Research and development	£2 000	
Sales and distribution	£2 000	
Finance	£1 000	
		£18 000
Trading profit		£2 000

It would be useful to express each of the expenses and the trading profit as a percentage of sales.

Table 2.1 is a suggested format for an operating statement. Here, the statement is produced monthly with a comparison between actual and planned figures for the relevant month and for the year to date. In this presentation sales revenue is expressed as 100 per cent and the costs and profit figures expressed as percentage of sales revenue.

Table 2.1 Operating statement

| | This month | | | | | | Year to date | | | | | |
| | Actual | | Budget | | Variance | | Actual | | Budget | | Variance | |
	£	%	£	%	£	%	£	%	£	%	£	%
Sales units												
Sales revenues	100		100				100		100			
Less direct costs:												
Materials												
Labour												
Other direct costs												
Total direct costs												
Gross profit												
Less indirect expenses:												
Production												
Administration												
Sales and distribution												
Research and development												
Finance												
Total expenses												
Trading profit												

Notes:
1 'Sales units' would be relevant where the company produces one or similar products. With a range of products it would make sense to produce a breakdown of the statement over the different products. This would be relatively easy to do with the sales units, the sales revenues and the direct costs, but problems arise when allocating the indirect expenses to the different products (see Chapter 3, where absorption, marginal and activity based costing are considered).
2 The direct costs are those directly related to the sales and will be affected by the changes in stock levels. Stocks may include raw materials, work in progress and finished goods. The accuracy of the month-end stock figures will affect the accuracy of the operating statement.

Questions that should be addressed are:
- how should the physical units of stock be converted into £ terms?
- should work-in-progress and finished goods stock include indirect costs as well as direct costs, and, if so, which ones? Most companies include an element of production indirect expenses in these stocks but tend to 'write off' the other overheads in the operating statement for the month in question.

Table 2.2 is an example of a summary balance sheet, again produced monthly. Probably only the current assets and current liabilities will show

Table 2.2   Summary balance sheet

	This month	Last month	% change
Fixed assets			
Land and buildings			
Plant and machinery			
Fixtures and fittings			
Motor vehicles			
Total fixed assets			
Investments			
Current assets			
Stocks			
Debtors			
Cash			
Total current assets			
Current liabilities			
Creditors			
Tax			
Overdraft			
Total current liabilities			
Net current assets			
Long-term liabilities			
Net assets			
Financed by:			
Share capital			
Reserves			
Shareholders' funds			

much movement month by month. The longer-term assets and liabilities tend to remain somewhat static.

EXERCISE

The directors of Timberland Ltd produce an operating statement, breaking the figures down over the two main product groups, tables and chairs.
The summarised operating statement for March is as follows:

	Tables (£000s)	Chairs (£000s)	Total (£000s)
Sales	300	200	500
Less direct costs	150	150	300
Gross profit	150	50	200
Less expenses	50	50	100
Trading profit	100	0	100

Which of the following decisions might the directors consider in the light of the above?

1   Drop chairs and sell only tables.
2   Increase the selling price of chairs.
3   Reduce the costs of chairs.
4   Reduce the selling price of chairs.
5   Consider the allocation of the expenses.

Some thoughts

1   Dropping chairs would mean losing £50 000 of gross profit, a *contribution* towards the expenses of the business. Dropping chairs would not necessarily mean a drop in the overall expenses. Would sales of tables be affected if chairs were not available?
2   What are competitors' prices for similar chairs? Raising the selling price of chairs would probably lead to a reduction in volume with a corresponding reduction in gross profit.
3   Could the direct materials be purchased more cheaply? Could cheaper substitute materials be used? Could quantity or prompt payment discounts be negotiated?
4   Reducing the selling price of chairs should lead to an increase in volume. Indirect expenses would not tend to rise and there could be an overall increase in the trading profit.
5   How have the indirect expenses been allocated to the products? A 50/50 split seems unfair.

3 Cost, profit and break-even

This chapter considers the three main methods of costing: **absorption costing, marginal costing** and **activity based costing**. **Costing** means establishing the cost of a product, service or department but also includes the concepts of cost control and cost reduction as well as cost behaviour patterns.

The cost of a product or service is often the basis for its selling price. Management's perception as to the relative profitability of different products might be based on misconceptions of 'cost'.

Costing has many functions including measuring, decision making, presentational and political. Different functions require different figures. Therefore, there are different costs for different purposes.

The chapter will also consider the calculation of break-even as well as cost, volume and profit analysis.

Absorption costing

In absorption costing (also known as total costing or full costing), *all* the overheads of the business are spread over the products using some predetermined bases.

The Timberland operating statement for March on page 29, provides an illustration of these bases. This is an example of absorption costing where the indirect expenses have been spread over the two products on a 50/50 basis. One method of spreading overheads is to use direct costs, for example:

Estimated direct costs for the year		£6m
Estimated overheads for the year		£2m
Absorption rate = £2m/£6m	=	33.3%

The accuracy of the absorption rate figure would be determined by the accuracy in estimating the direct costs and the overheads. If these are wrong, then the absorption rate is wrong.

In any event, is there a relationship between the direct costs and the indirects? In the example, the overheads have been absorbed into the costs of production on the basis of the estimated direct costs for the year. Is this a valid basis for recovering overheads? It is unlikely that the level of overheads (indirects) bears much relationship to the incidence of direct costs.

Use of the absorption rate

The predetermined rate is applied to actual direct costs as follows:

Job 1234:	£
Total direct costs	30 000
Overhead recovery (30 000 × 33.3%)	10 000
Cost of job	40 000

At the end of the year the overheads recovered using the absorption rate figure should be compared with the actual overheads incurred to see whether the former are more than the latter (over-recovery) or vice-versa (under-recovery). Over-recovery would be an addition to the management accounting profit whilst under-recovery would be a reduction. The greater the over- or under-recovery, the greater the inaccuracy in estimating the overheads and the direct costs.

The four stages in absorption costing are:

1 estimate overheads for year
2 allocate those overheads that can be directly related to departments
3 apportion remaining overheads to departments
4 absorb overheads into products.

Table 3.1 shows an example of absorption costing. The overheads in this table have been allocated and apportioned to three production departments and will be absorbed into the production units on the basis of estimated machine hours for department 1, a machine shop, estimated labour, hours for department 2, an assembly department, and on the number of units passing through department 3, a paint shop.

Other bases used to absorb overheads into product costs include estimated labour costs, estimated material costs and estimated total direct costs (known as prime costs). For example:

Table 3.1 Absorption costing

Production overheads	Spread Method	Dept. 1	Dept. 2	Dept. 3	Total
		£	£	£	£
Rent and rates	Floor area	3 000	4 000	5 000	12 000
Heat and light	Floor area	3 000	4 000	5 000	12 000
Power	Metered	9 000	10 000	13 000	32 000
Insurance	Value	1 000	1 000	2 000	4 000
Depreciation	Value	9 000	12 000	18 000	39 000
Telephone	No. of extns.	1 000	1 000	2 000	4 000
Canteen	No. of employees	3 000	4 000	5 000	12 000
Salaries:					
Supervisors	Allocated	8 000	9 000	10 000	27 000
Production manager	No. of employees	10 000	11 000	12 000	33 000
Stores	No. of requisitions	5 000	3 000	5 000	13 000
Maintenance	No. of hours spent	5 000	8 000	7 000	20 000
Totals		57 000	67 000	84 000	208 000
Estimated machine hours		28 500			
Estimated labour hours			67 000		
Estimated production in units				168 000	
Absorption rates		£2/hour	£1/hour	50p/unit	

Table 3.2 An example of total cost arrived at by using absorption costing

	£	
Direct material cost	50	Accuracy determined by the physical
Direct labour cost	60	controls in the works
Direct expenses	20	
Prime cost	130	
Indirect works cost	30	
Manufacturing cost	160	Accuracy determined by guesswork
Indirect admin. cost	16	
Cost of production	176	
Indirect sales and distribution	30	
Total cost	206	

Notes:
1 Examples of direct expenses include royalties, packaging and depreciation of a machine used solely on the above product
2 Administration overheads are often absorbed (recovered) on the basis of estimated manufacturing cost, for example:

estimated admin. overheads	£300 000
estimated manufacturing cost	£3 000 000

   absorption rate = 10% of manufacturing cost
3 Selling and distribution overheads are often recovered on the basis of estimated sales, for example:

estimated S & D overheads	£400 000
estimated sales	£4 000 000

   absorption rates = 10% of sales

Estimated labour costs for Dept C: £150 000
Estimated overheads for Dept C: £300 000
Therefore recovery rate = £2 of overhead for every £1 of labour cost.

There should be some connection between the activity of the department and the choice of recovery rate.

In Table 3.2, the indirect costs – £30, £16 and £30 – have been 'absorbed' into the cost of the product, (£206). However, if the selling price were to be set at, say, £300, the true profit is unlikely to be £94 per unit because the indirect costs, amounting to £76, have been estimated ('guesstimated') using bases which are of doubtful accuracy.

EXERCISE

A product, X, has a direct material cost of £50, direct labour cost of £60 and direct expenses of £20. Machine hour time in department 1 was 6, labour hours in department 2 amounted to 17½ and the product was painted.
Calculate the works overheads recovered.

ANSWER

Dept 1:	6 × £2 =	£12.00
Dept 2:	17½ × £1 =	£17.50
Dept 3:	1 unit × 50p =	£ 0.50
		£30.00

Questions for management to ask

When managers are presented with figures for the 'cost' of products, services, jobs or contracts, the following questions should be considered if absorption costing is to be used:

1 How are the indirects spread over the departments?
2 How are the indirects absorbed into the products?
3 How often are over/under-recoveries to be checked?
4 How are these treated in the accounts?
5 How are administration, selling and distribution overheads included in product costs?
6 How are the HO costs spread over departments? In some companies the more sales a department achieves, the more HO overheads are allocated to that department. One manager, who realised that HO expenses were allocated on the basis of direct labour hours, redeployed some direct labourers as indirects so reducing the burden of the HO allocation and boosting his departmental profit.

Summary

If an organisation is using absorption costing, the 'cost' of individual products is probably wrong. The more products and the more 'cost centre' departments there are, the more inaccurate the product costs become. Managers should be wary of making decisions based on absorption costing and 'total cost' should never be used as the basis of selling price.

The accuracy of the total cost figure is determined by the accuracy of the estimates used in arriving at the recovery rates.

EXERCISE

Consider the following:

Estimated overheads	£800 000
Estimated production (units)	400 000
Recovery rate = £2 per unit	
Direct cost of products – £10 per unit	

Calculate the unit total cost if actual production was

- 200 000 units
- 400 000 units
- 800 000 units

Assume the actual overheads were £800 000.

ANSWER

Production	Direct cost/unit £	Overhead cost/unit £	Total cost/unit £
200 000	10	4	14
400 000	10	2	12
800 000	10	1	11

Notice how the total cost per unit changes with changes in volume. At 200 000 units of production the selling price would have to exceed £14 to make a profit, whilst at 800 000 units of production the selling price would have to exceed £11. If the selling price as determined by the market is £12 per unit then production and sales would have to exceed 400 000 units to make a profit.

EXERCISE

In a restaurant business, the variable costs are the cost of the food and drink which average out to £5 per customer. The fixed costs, the rent, rates, wages and so on, amount to £1000 per week.

What is the unit cost of one, ten, 50 and 100 meals per week?

ANSWER

No. of meals	Variable cost £	Fixed cost £	Cost/meal £
1	5	1000	1005
10	50	1000	105
50	250	1000	25
100	500	1000	15

EXERCISE

Draw a graph showing cost/meal on the y axis and number of customers on the x axis.

ANSWER

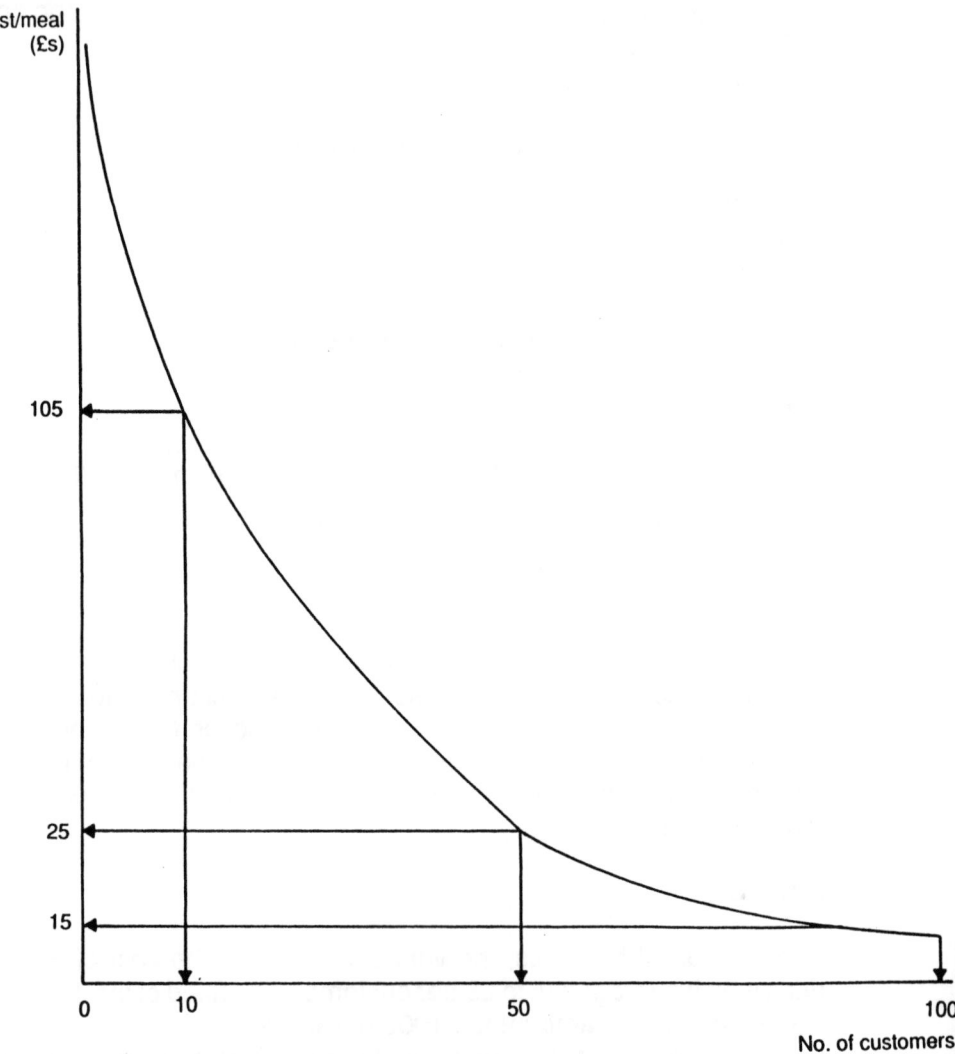

Figure 3.1   Cost per meal according to number of customers

As demonstrated in Figure 3.1, the cost per meal is clearly affected by the number of customers. The fixed costs, which remain the same, are spread over a greater number of units.

If the number of customers was predicted to be 50 per week, the selling price per meal would have to be more than £25 to make a profit. If it was exactly £25 the business would break even.

Reducing the price of a meal would probably attract more customers. If the price was reduced to £15, the total number of customers would have to exceed 100 if the business was to make a profit.

Peanuts – a moral story, American-style

The following story illustrates the dangers of using absorption costing and attempting to load every activity with its share of overheads.

Joe, the restaurateur, adds a rack of peanuts to the counter, hoping to pick up a little extra profit in the usual course of business. He is interviewed by his Accountant-Efficiency-Expert.

Eff. Ex. Joe, you said you put in these peanuts because some people ask for them, but do you realise what this rack of peanuts is costing you?

Joe It ain't gonna cost. 'Sgonna be a profit. Sure, I hadda pay $25 for a fancy rack to holda bags, but the peanuts cost 6c a bag and I sell 'em for 10c. Figger I sell 50 bags a week to start. It'll take 12½ weeks to cover the cost of the rack. After that I gotta clear profit of 4c a bag. The more I sell, the more I make.

Eff. Ex. That is an antiquated and completely unrealistic approach, Joe. Fortunately, modern accounting procedures permit a more accurate picture which reveals the complexities involved.

Joe. Huh?

Eff. Ex. To be precise, those peanuts must be integrated into your entire operation and be allocated their appropriate share of business overhead. They must share a proportionate part of your expenditures for rent, heat, light, equipment depreciation, decorating, salaries for your waitresses, cook . . . .

Joe The cook? What'sa he gotta do wit'a peanuts? He don't even know I got 'em!

Eff. Ex. Look, Joe, the cook is in the kitchen, the kitchen prepares the food, the food is what brings people in here, and the people ask to buy peanuts. That's why you must charge a portion of the cook's wages, as well as part of your own salary to peanut sales. This sheet contains a carefully calculated costs analysis which indicates the peanut operation should pay exactly $1278 per year toward these general overhead costs.

Joe The peanuts? $1278 a year for overhead? The nuts?

Eff. Ex. It's really a little more than that. You also spend money each week to have the windows washed, to have the place swept out in the mornings and keep soap in the washroom. That raises the total to $1813 per year.

Joe (Thoughtfully) But the peanut salesman said I'd make money . . . put 'em on the end of the counter, he said . . . and get 4c a bag profit.

Eff. Ex. (With a sniff) He's not an accountant. Do you actually know what the portion of the counter occupied by the peanut rack is worth to you?

Joe Ain't worth nothing. No stool there . . . just a dead spot at the end.

Eff. Ex. The modern cost picture permits no dead spots. Your counter contains 60 square feet and your counter business grosses $15 000 a year. Consequently, the square foot of space occupied by the peanut rack is worth $250 per year. Since you have taken that area away from general counter use, you must charge the value of the space to the occupant.

Joe   You mean I gotta add $250 a year more to the peanuts?

Eff. Ex.   Right. That raises their share of the general operating costs to a grand total of $2063 per year. Now then, if you sell 50 bags of peanuts per week, these allocated costs will amount to 41c per bag.

Joe   WHAT?

Eff. Ex.   Obviously, to that must be added your purchase price of 6c per bag, which brings the total to 47c. So you see, by selling peanuts at 10c per bag you are losing 37c on every sale.

Joe   Somethin's crazy!

Eff. Ex.   Not at all. Here are the figures. They prove your peanut operation cannot stand on its own feet.

Joe   (Brightening) Suppose I sell lotsa peanuts . . . thousand bags a week 'stead of fifty?

Eff. Ex.   (Tolerantly) Joe, you don't understand the problem. If the volume of peanut sales increases, your operating costs will go up . . . you'll have to handle more bags, with more time, more depreciation, more everything. The basic principle of accounting is firm on that subject! 'The Bigger the Operation the More General Overhead Costs that Must be Allocated'. No, increasing the volume of sales won't help.

Joe   Okay. You so smart, you tell me what I gotta do.

Eff. Ex.   (Condescendingly) Well . . . you could first reduce operating expenses.

Joe   How?

Eff. Ex.   Move to a building with cheaper rent. Cut salaries. Wash the windows bi-weekly. Have the floor swept only on Thursday. Remove the soap from the washrooms. Decrease the square foot value of your counter. For example, if you can cut your expenses 50 per cent that will reduce the amount allocated to peanuts from $2063 down to $1051.50 per year, reducing the cost to 21c per bag.

Joe   (Slowly) That's better?

Eff. Ex.   Much, much better. However, even then you would lose 11c per bag if you charge only 10c. Therefore, you must also raise your selling price. If you want a net profit of 4c per bag you would have to charge 25c.

Joe   (Flabbergasted) You mean even after I cut operating costs 50 per cent, I still gotta charge 25c for a 10c bag of peanuts? Nobody's nuts about nuts! Who'd buy 'em?

Eff. Ex.   That's a secondary consideration. The point is, at 25c you'd be selling at a price based upon a true and proper evaluation of your then reduced costs.

Joe   (Eagerly) Look! I gotta better idea. Why don't I just throw the nuts out . . . put 'em in an ash can?

Eff. Ex.   Can you afford it?

Joe   Sure. All I got is about 50 bags of peanuts . . . cost about three bucks . . . so I lost $25 on the rack, but I'm outa this nasty business and no more grief.

Eff. Ex.   (Shaking head) Joe it isn't quite that simple. You are in the peanut business! The minute you throw those peanuts out you are adding $2063 of the annual overhead to the rest of your operation. Joe . . . be realistic . . . can you afford to do that?

Joe   (Completely crushed) It'sa unbelievable! Last I was a make money. Now I'm in a trouble . . . justa because I think peanuts on a counter is gonna bring me some extra profit . . . justa because I believe 50 bags of peanuts a week is a easy.

Eff. Ex.   (With raised eyebrow) That is the object of modern cost studies, Joe . . . to dispel those false illusions.

Marginal costing

Marginal costing includes in product costs only those costs which vary with activity – the variable costs – which include direct materials, power and commissions. Fixed costs are excluded from the product costs and are usually paid out of the contributions generated by the sale of the products.

Contribution is the difference between sales and variable costs. Hitherto this has been referred to as 'gross profit'. Contribution per unit is the difference between the sale price of that unit and its variable cost. The terms variable cost and marginal cost are synonymous.

Looking again at the profit and loss account of Timberland Ltd on pages 28–9, the marginal costing presentation is shown in Table 3.3.

Table 3.3   Marginal costing

	Tables	Chairs	Total
Sales	300 000	200 000	500 000
Less cost of goods sold (variable)	150 000	150 000	300 000
Contribution	150 000	50 000	200 000
Less fixed costs			100 000
Trading profit			100 000

The fixed costs are not 'allocated' to the product groups but remain as a single entity. The aim is now to make enough contributions to pay the fixed costs and leave some over for profit.

The profitability of the two product groups can be expressed as the percentage of contribution to sales, that is:

Tables	Chairs	Total
50%	25%	40%

This percentage of contribution to sales is also known as the **P/V ratio** (a bit of a misnomer perhaps because P stands for 'profit' and V for 'volume').

Contribution per unit

Table 3.4 considers the marginal cost of product H. The sale of each unit contributed £50 to the 'contribution fund' out of which the fixed costs are paid. The remainder, if there is any, is profit.

The P/V ratio of product is:

contribution/sales as a percentage
$$= 50/350 \times 100\%$$
$$= 14.3\%$$

The danger with marginal costing is that management might get into the routine of pricing products on the basis of very low contributions in the hope of undercutting the competition or boosting volume.

In the final analysis

Sales – costs = profit

Table 3.4 Illustration of the marginal cost of a product

	£
Direct material cost	100
Direct labour cost	100
Direct expense	50
Prime cost	250
Variable overhead:	
power, commission, freight	50
Marginal cost	300
Contribution	50
Selling price	350

Splitting costs into their fixed and variable elements does not alter this basic equation.

The story goes that two New Yorkers were trying to outdo each other regarding the price they had paid for identical watches.

'I got this watch for $50 wholesale. How much did you pay?'

'I paid $25 for the same watch. That's below cost.'

'Below cost! How the hell does the guy make a profit?'

'He sells a lot of watches.'

Uses of marginal costing

Elimination of competition

Two companies, A and B, sell product G. A sells many products whilst B sells only G.

The cost structure of G is as follows:

	Co. A £	Co. B £
Total absorbed cost	10	8
Profit	2	2
Selling price	12	10

If price is the overriding factor then Co. B will dominate the market in sales of G.

Co. A decides to re-analyse its costs and discovers the following:

	£
Fixed cost/unit	5
Variable cost/unit	5
Total cost	10

What price should Co. A charge for G so as to maximise its profit and eliminate Co. B?

The selling price/unit should be £8. This gives a contribution of £8 – £5 = £3 (sales price less variable cost). Co. A can recover its fixed costs from the contributions from all its products, but Co. B may find its freedom to manoeuvre limited.

Fixing prices in times of recession and depression

In times of recession and depression, reducing selling prices should help to stimulate demand. The bench-mark for fixing the minimum price would be the marginal cost.

Using the example above, any price above £5 would generate some contribution. Marketing should estimate the different volumes that would be sold at the different prices and choose the price that would maximise total contributions, for example,

Price/ unit £	Variable costs £	Contribution £	Volume	Total Contribution £
8	5	3	50 000	150 000 (50 000 × 3)
7	5	2	80 000	160 000 (80 000 × 2)
6	5	1	100 000	100 000 (100 000 × 1)

Using idle capacity

With underutilised floor space or labour, fixed costs are still being incurred. Ways of generating contributions to help pay these fixed costs include 'own label' brands of 'brand label switch' where products are sold at reduced selling prices which nevertheless give rise to increased contributions.

Loss leaders

Selling one product at a much lower P/V ratio than the others may help to boost sales not only of the loss leader but of the more profitable products also. The danger is that the budgeted product mix is not achieved and too much of the loss leader is sold.

The profitability of products using marginal costing

Consider the following data relating to four products:

Product	A	B	C	D
Sales price	£15	£20	£30	£40
Marginal cost	£12	£15	£20	£25
Contribution	£3	£5	£10	£15
P/V ratio	20%	25%	33.33%	37.5%

Using the P/V ratio for ranking the products the order would be:

- 1 – D
- 2 – C
- 3 – B
- 4 – A.

The products should be produced in that order to meet the demand for each product. This would be fine if there was no constraint on the production of these products. Suppose, however, that there was a factor limiting the output of the firm such as machine capacity, availability of skilled labour, special material, floor space or sales demand. These are known as **key** or **limiting factors**. Management's task is now to maximise the **contribution per limiting factor**.

Suppose that the firm producing A, B, C and D has a key factor of 3000 machine hours per month. Fixed costs are £10 000 per month. Management wishes to maximise the profit by considering the demand for each product and the contributions per limiting factor.

	A	B	C	D
Contribution/unit	£3	£5	£10	£15
Machine hours/unit	0.5	0.75	2	5
Contribution/hour	£6	£6.67	£5	£3

The rankings would then be revised:

- 1 – B
- 2 – A
- 3 – C
- 4 – D.

The monthly demand for the products is:

- A – 1000 units
- B – 1000 units
- C – 500 units
- D – 500 units.

Management should meet the demand for each product in order of profitability remembering that the limiting factor is 3000 machine hours per month.

	Demand	Produce	Cont./ unit	Cont./ hour	Total. cont.	Machine hours
B	1000	1000	£5	£6.67	£5 000	750
A	1000	1000	£3	£6	£3 000	500
C	500	500	£10	£5	£5 000	1000
D	500	150	£15	£3	£2 250	750
					£15 250	3000
Fixed costs					£10 000	
Maximum profit					£5 520	

Note: Only 150 units of product D, the least profitable product, can be produced as only 750 out of the 3000 machine hours remain.

Marginal or absorption costing?

There is no 'right' answer as to which method should be adopted. Management should appreciate that the choice of method is dictated by a variety of factors. In any event, a new method has recently appeared on the costing scene – **activity based costing** (see page 58) – and this may, in certain circumstances, be more applicable than the two traditional methods. Table 3.5 summarises the features of marginal and absorption costing.

Table 3.5   Marginal and absorption costing

Marginal	Absorption
Useful in decision making	Stresses the importance of fixed costs
States that profit is a function of sales	States that profit is a function of both sales and production
Fixed costs are not included in stock valuations but are written off as period costs*	Fixed costs are included in stock valuations which will affect future profit and loss
To be preferred in a multi-product company	Relevant in a company with few products and where supply and demand can be predicted with reasonable accuracy
Useful in times of recession where there is idle capacity and in one-off special order situations	Where absorption rates are based on direct labour which has become a smaller proportion of total costs, the costing information may be flawed

*Those costs which arise in a particular period, irrespective of activity during that period. In marginal costing they are 'written off' – i.e. changed to the profit and loss account for that period. In absorption costing some of these costs may be carried over to future periods as part of stock valuation.

Summary

Absorption costing includes fixed and variable costs in product costs:

Sales	1000
Less costs	500
Profit	500

Marginal costing includes only variable costs in product costs:

Sales	1000
Less variable costs	300
Contribution	700
Less fixed costs	200
Profit	500

Break-even analysis

A break-even situation is when a business makes neither a profit nor a loss. It is the sales revenue that must be achieved before a profit is generated. It may also be expressed as the number of units that need to be sold before profits are made.

Cash break-even is when there is neither a surplus nor an overdraft.

In budgeting, the break-even point is a crucial figure in deciding the viability of projects and business plans.

Consider the following profit and loss statement for AB Wholesale Ltd.

	£	%
Sales	500 000	100
Less variable costs	300 000	60
Contribution	200 000	40
Less fixed costs	100 000	
Trading profit	100 000	

EXERCISE

What sales revenue figure has to be achieved for the business to break even?

ANSWER

On the face of it, reducing the sales figure by £100 000 to £400 000 would knock £100 000 off the profit. But consider the following:

	£	%
Sales	400 000	100
Less variable costs	240 000	60
Contribution	160 000	40
Less fixed costs	100 000	
Profit	60 000	

If sales are less, then variable costs will be less. The assumption is that variable costs remain at 60 per cent of sales whatever the sales figure.

The sales revenue figure that produces break-even must be the sales that give rise to a contribution of £100 000 because contribution − fixed costs = profit. If sales of £500 000 give a contribution of £200 000, then sales of £250 000 will give a contribution of £100 000. This means that the break-even figure is £250 000.

	£	%
Sales	250 000	100
Less variable costs	150 000	60
Contribution	100 000	40
Less fixed costs	100 000	
Trading profit	0	

The formula for calculating the break-even point is

fixed costs/PV ratio.

That is,

100 000/40%
= 250 000.

(Remember: P/V ratio = contribution/sales × 100%.)

This is the first key formula in break-even analysis.

Once the break-even point has been reached, the fixed costs have been exactly matched by the contributions from the sales. This means that sales above the break-even point will give a profit measured by the contributions from those sales.

The second formula, which gives the profit or loss at any sales figure, is:

profit = (sales − break-even) × P/V ratio

For example, if sales were £400 000, the profit for AB Wholesale Ltd would be

(£400 000 − £250 000) × 40%
= £150 000 × 40%
= £60 000

EXERCISE

What would the loss be if sales were £200 000?

ANSWER

Using the second key formula, that is

   profit = (sales – break-even) × P/V ratio

we find that the loss is

   (£200 000 – £250 000) × 40%
   = (£20 000) loss.

Break-even chart

The break-even chart of AB Wholesale Ltd (Figure 3.2) introduces the sales revenue line to the diagram of fixed, variable and total costs. The point on

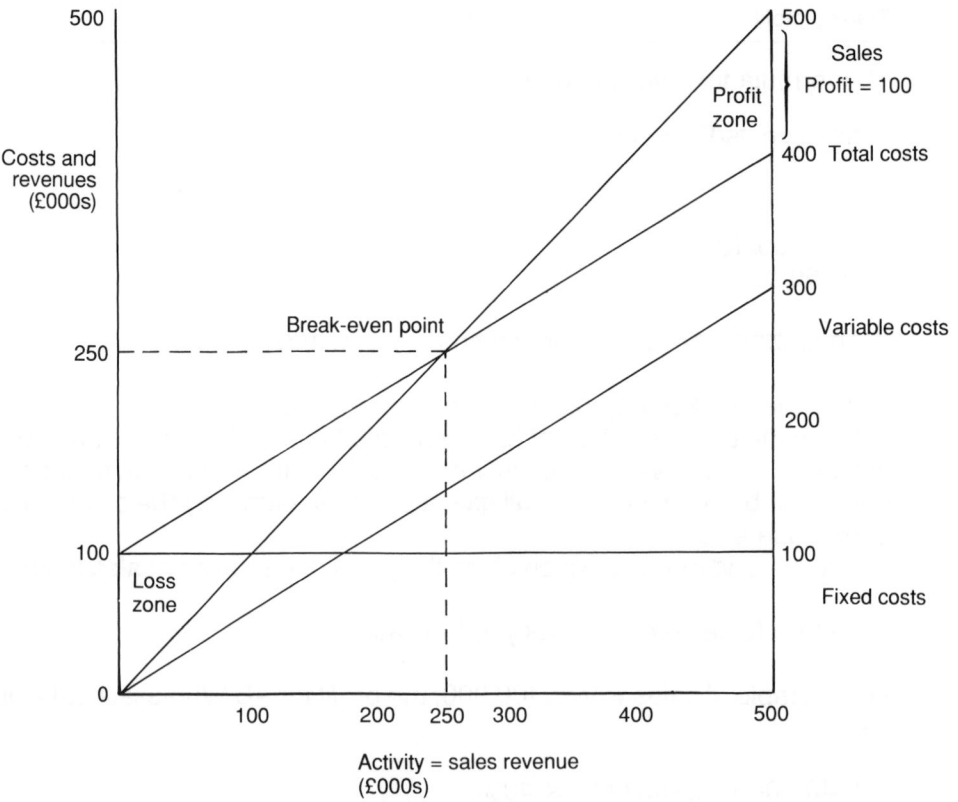

Figure 3.2   Break-even chart

the break-even chart where the sales revenue line and the total cost line meet is the break-even point (known in France as *'le point de mort'*). The figure here is, of course, £250 000.

The profit at any sales level above £250 000 can be measured in the 'profit zone' as the distance between sales revenue and total costs. At sales of £500 000 the profit can be measured as £100 000.

The loss at any sales revenue figure below £250 000 is measured in the 'loss zone' by the distance between the total cost line and the sales line. At sales of £200 000 the loss is shown to be £20 000.

Margin of safety

The difference between the budgeted sales and the break-even figure is known as the margin of safety. It is normally expressed as a percentage, that is the percentage drop from the budgeted sales that would give rise to a loss situation.

In AB Wholesale Ltd, for example, if the budgeted sales were £750 000 and the break-even was £250 000, then the margin of safety would be £750 000 – £250 000 = £500 000, or expressed as a percentage:

£500 000/£750 000 = 66.7%

A margin of safety below 30 per cent would indicate a high risk situation.

Problems in establishing break-even

It is not always true that fixed costs remain fixed irrespective of the level of activity. To increase activity over certain levels may require additional fixed costs. These tend to increase in steps and are called **stepped fixed costs**. Their effect on the break-even chart is demonstrated in Figure 3.3 which shows three break-even points with loss and profit zones appearing at different stages in the activity levels.

The following points about break-even charts should be noted:

- The lines are not necessarily straight.
- Sales price per unit may have to be reduced at high levels of supply and larger customers may be entitled to quantity of discounts.
- If demand outweighs supply, it might be feasible to increase unit selling prices.
- Material cost per unit may also reduce with large purchases or may increase with shortages.
- Labour cost per unit will probably reduce at higher production levels.
- All costs are variable in the long term.
- Both fixed and variable costs will tend to increase with time.
- Costs do not always split conveniently between fixed and variable.
- The mix of products may change.

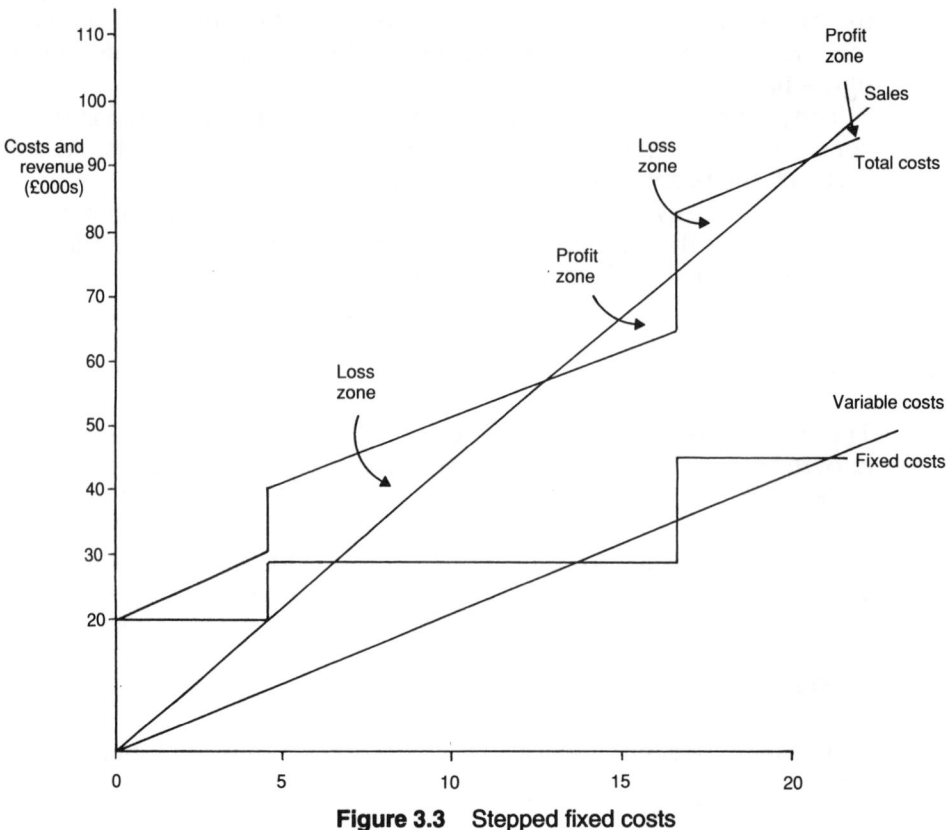

Figure 3.3   Stepped fixed costs

Relevant range

Accountants only seem to be able to draw straight lines while economists draw them curved (curvilinear). Accountants argue that we should be interested in what happens in the normal areas of activity, or relevant range. If the relevant range, as determined by our minimum and maximum levels of activity, is not too wide, then drawing straight lines should be a fair representation of what happens in practice (see Figure 3.4).

Profit improvement

There are only five ways of improving profitability in a business:

1   increasing sales prices
2   reducing variable costs
3   reducing fixed costs
4   improving product mix
5   increasing sales volume

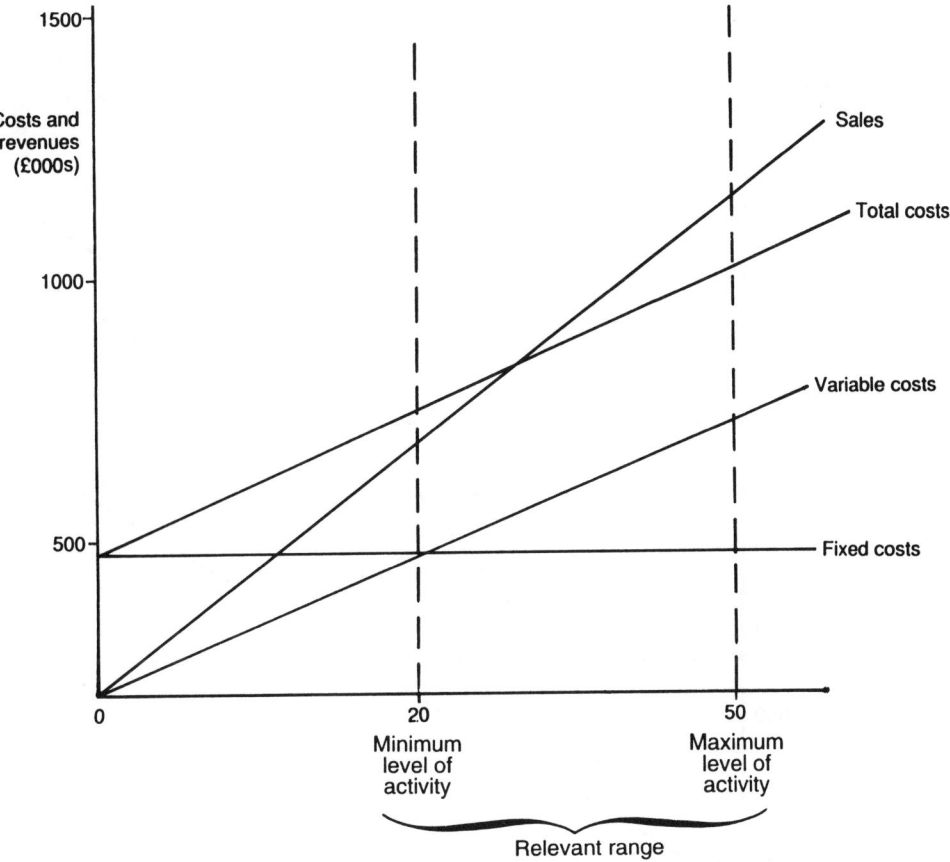

Figure 3.4   Relevant range

The effect of the above on break-even and profit and loss zones is illustrated by the break-even charts in Figures 3.5–3.10.

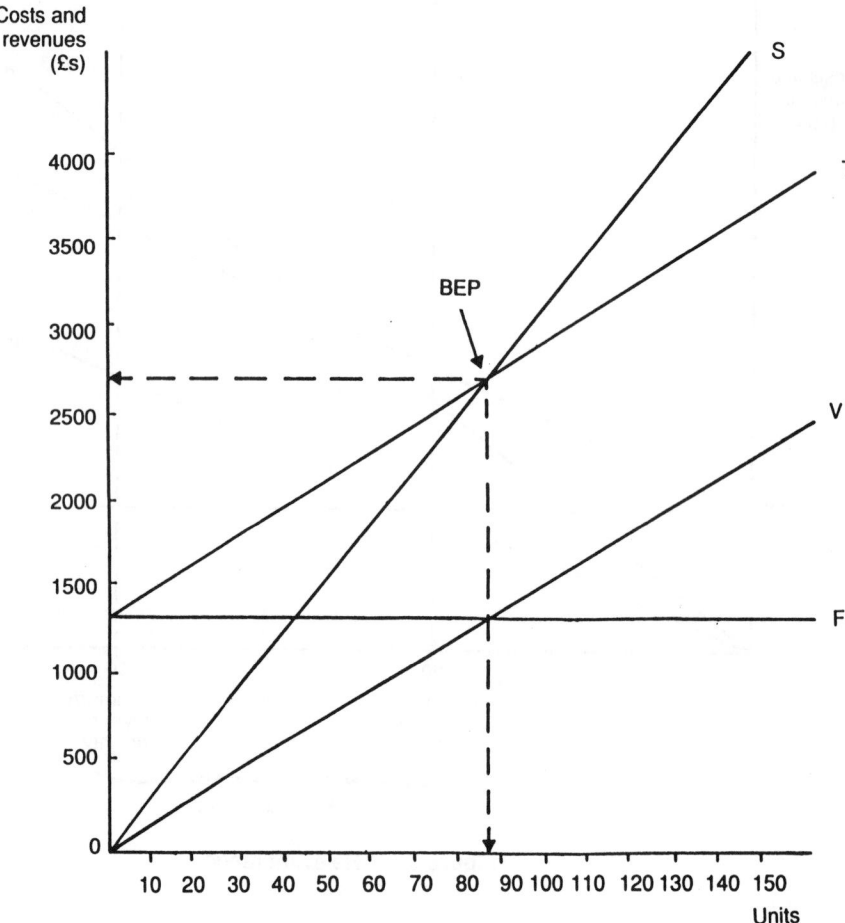

Figure 3.5   Original break-even chart

In Figure 3.5 a company has fixed costs of £1300, sales of £4480 (140 units) and a break-even of £2752 (86 units) per week.

The directors wish to establish the effect of price increases, cost reductions and volume changes.

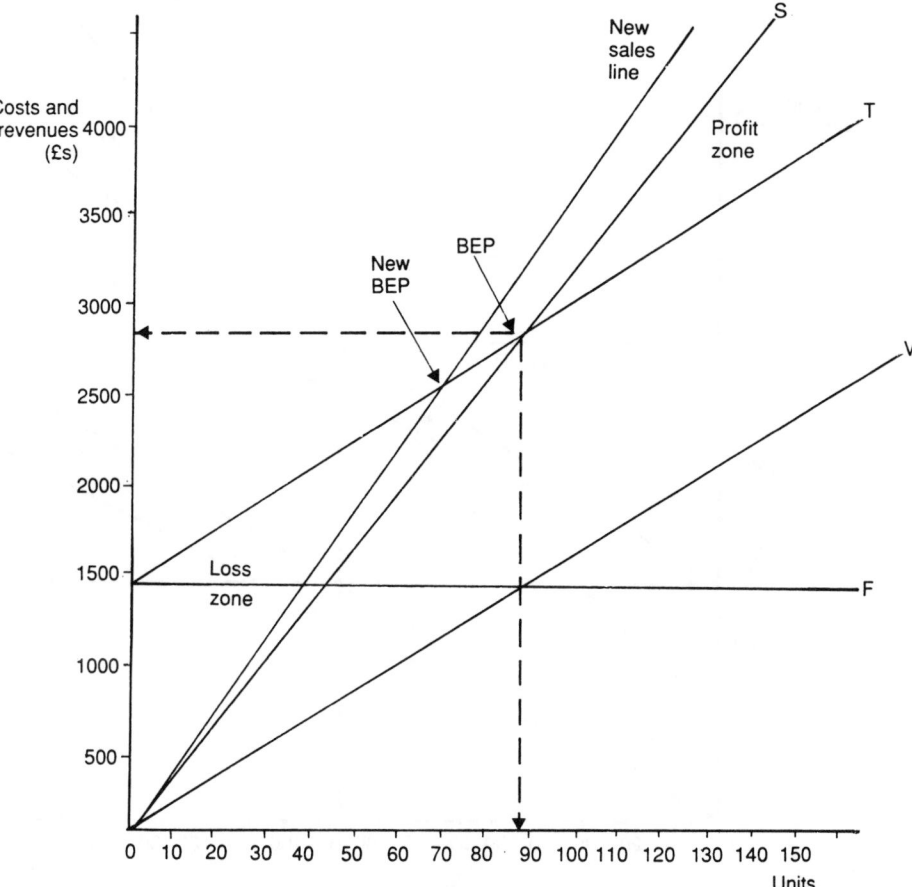

Figure 3.6   Revised break-even chart showing the effects of price increases

Here, by increasing the selling price, the break-even point has been reduced, the loss zone diminished and the profit zone increased. However, the effect on demand of such a policy must be considered. How does the revised price compare with competitors' prices?

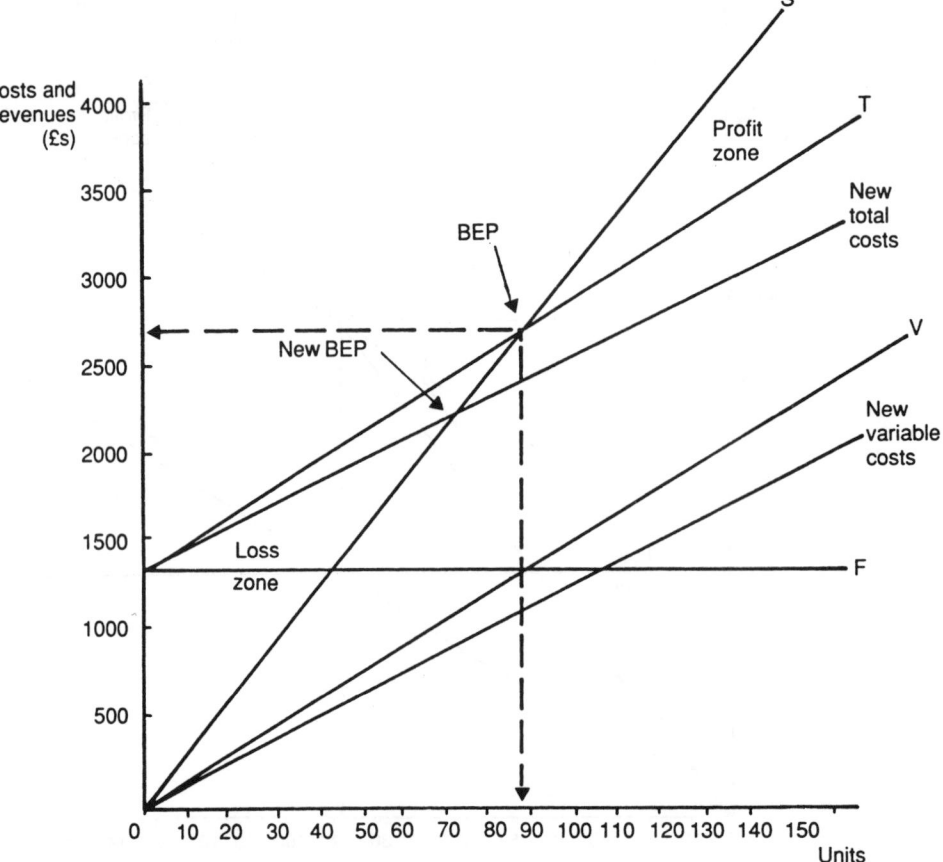

Figure 3.7 Revised break-even chart showing the effects of reducing variable costs

Here, by reducing variable costs, the break-even point has been reduced, the loss zone diminished and the profit zone increased.
    Ways of reducing variable costs include:

- using cheaper, substitute materials
- employing labour more efficiently
- increasing volume of production and obtaining quantity discounts
- paying for materials more quickly and getting prompt payment discount.

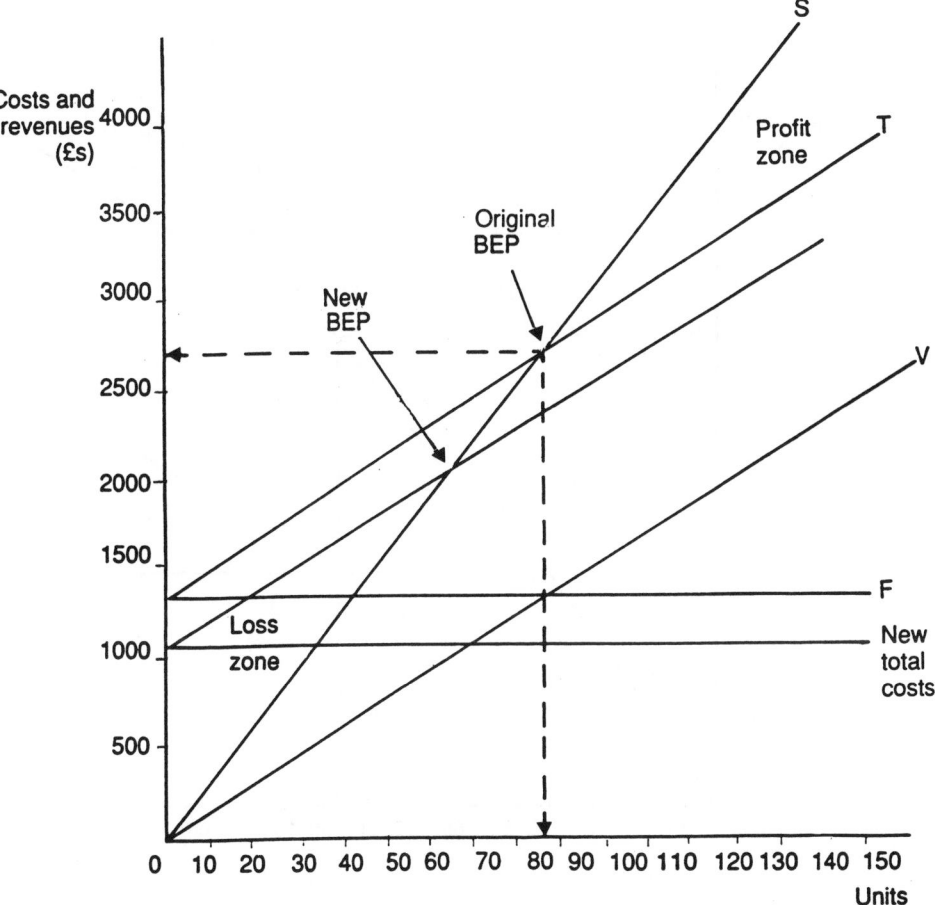

Figure 3.8   Revised break-even chart showing the effects of reducing fixed costs

By reducing fixed costs the break-even point has been reduced, the loss zone diminished and the profit zone increased.

Ways of reducing fixed costs include:

- moving to cheaper or smaller premises
- reducing the number of salaried staff
- cutting back on advertising, training and other discretionary costs
- reducing travelling expenses
- reducing interest costs by reducing investment in stocks and debtors or increasing payment times to suppliers.

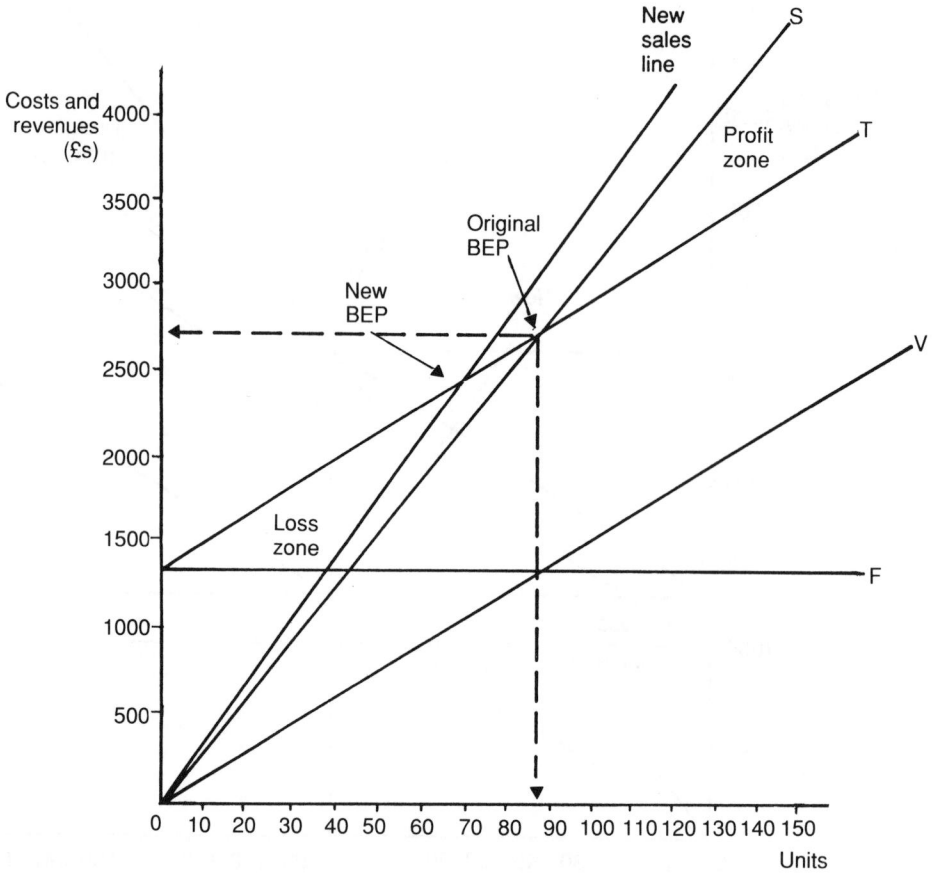

Figure 3.9   Revised break-even chart showing the effects of changing the product mix

By changing the product mix and selling more of the higher margin products, the break-even point has been reduced, the loss zone diminished and the profit zone increased.

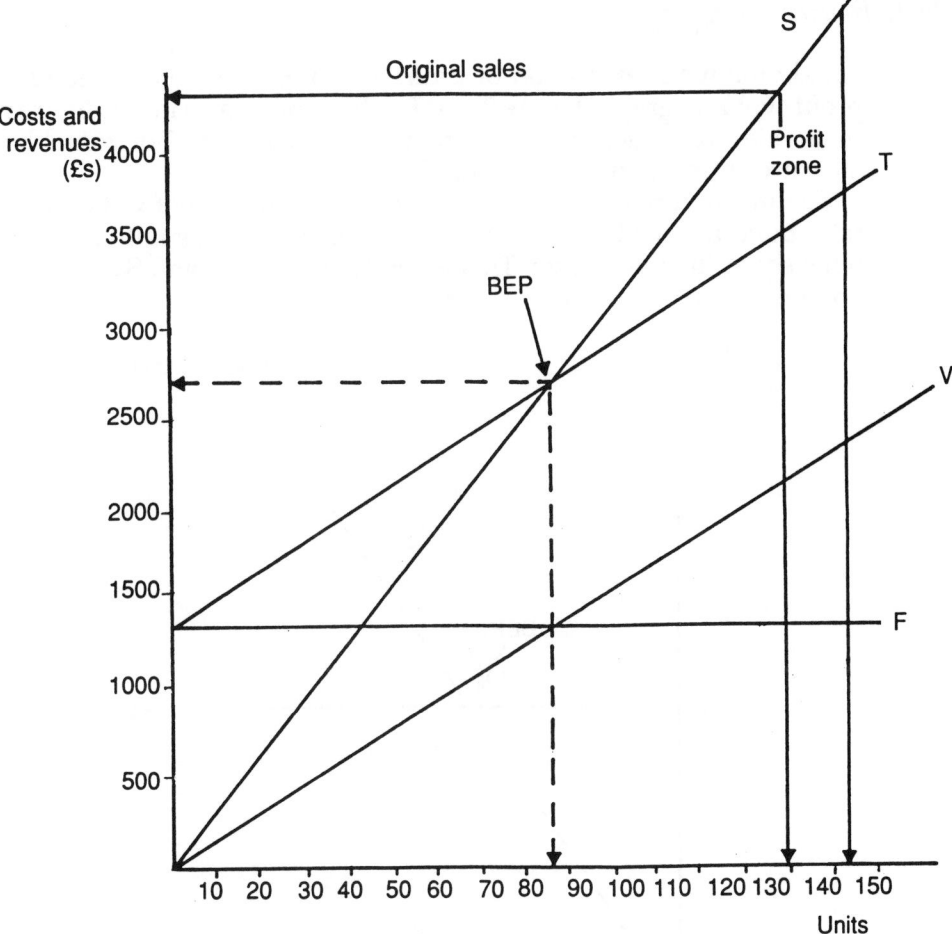

Figure 3.10   Revised break-even chart showing the effects of increasing sales volume

By increasing sales volume the break-even point remains the same as does the loss zone, but the profit zone increases.
Sales volume can be increased by

- increasing advertising (increase in fixed costs)
- increasing number of salesmen (increase in fixed costs)
- reducing selling prices.

Questions to consider are:

- Does the company have the production capacity?
- What will the effect be on cash flow?
- Is there a market for the increased production?

Profit/volume graph

An alternative presentation of profit and break-even is provided by the profit/volume graph (Figure 3.11). The horizontal axis in this figure represents sales (revenues or units). The distance above the horizontal line is a measure of profit and the distance below, of loss.

The maximum loss, when sales are zero, will be the fixed costs (F). As sales build up, the loss is reduced by the contributions until the contributions equal the fixed costs. This is the break-even point. Sales above this point contribute towards the profit.

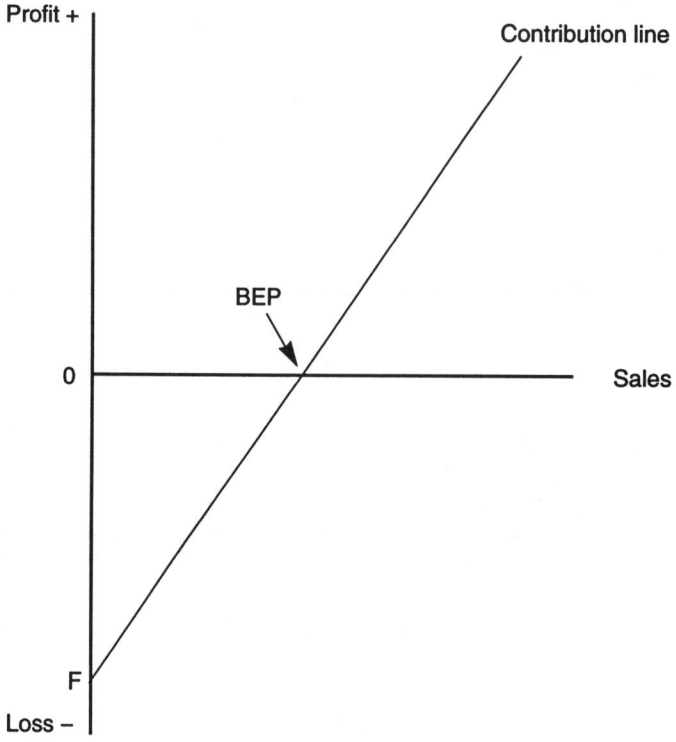

Figure 3.11 Profit/volume graph

Management might prefer this presentation when considering, for example, the effect on profit and break-even of different prices for the same product or the effect of different product mixes.

Suppose marketing are considering the introduction of a new product and have forecast the following demands at the alternative prices:

	£10	£12	£15
Selling price	£10	£12	£15
Marginal cost	£7	£7	£7
Contribution	£3	£5	£8
Demand (000s)	100	80	40
Total contribution (£000s)	300	400	320

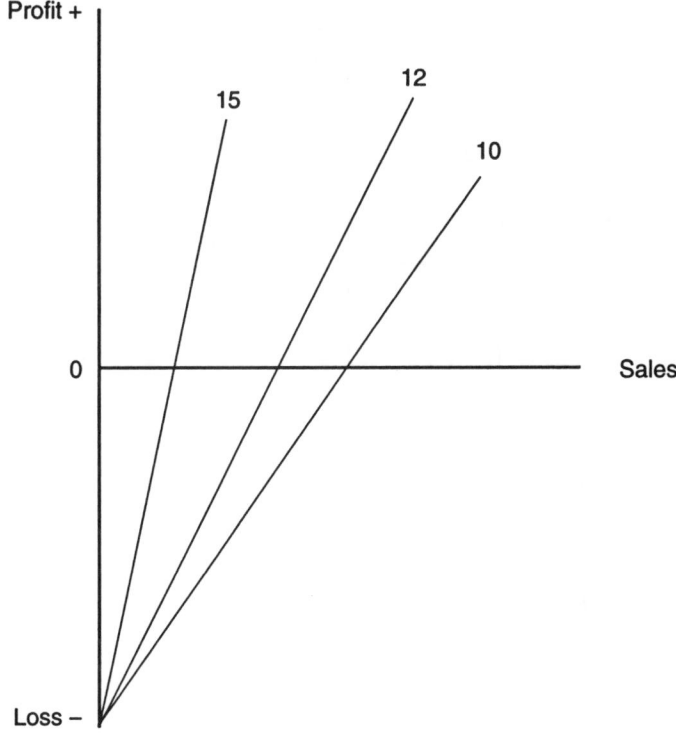

Figure 3.12   Profit/volume graph

These different scenarios can be expressed on a profit/volume graph as in Figure 3.12.

A sequential profit/volume graph will show the contributions made by different divisions, departments or product groups.

In the business represented in Figure 3.13, department 1 is the most profitable (as shown by the steepness of the contribution line), with department 2 the next most profitable and department 3 the least profitable. The break-even points and profits from department 1 and departments 1, 2 and 3 can be measured from the chart.

High fixed and high variable cost businesses

High fixed costs

Break-even is reached at a much higher volume than in a business with high variable costs. Once break-even is reached, the rate of profit contribution is much higher.

The margin of safety is likely to be much lower. The jargon for this is **operational leverage**. Operational leverage will be much higher for the high fixed cost business.

High fixed cost businesses will tend to have:

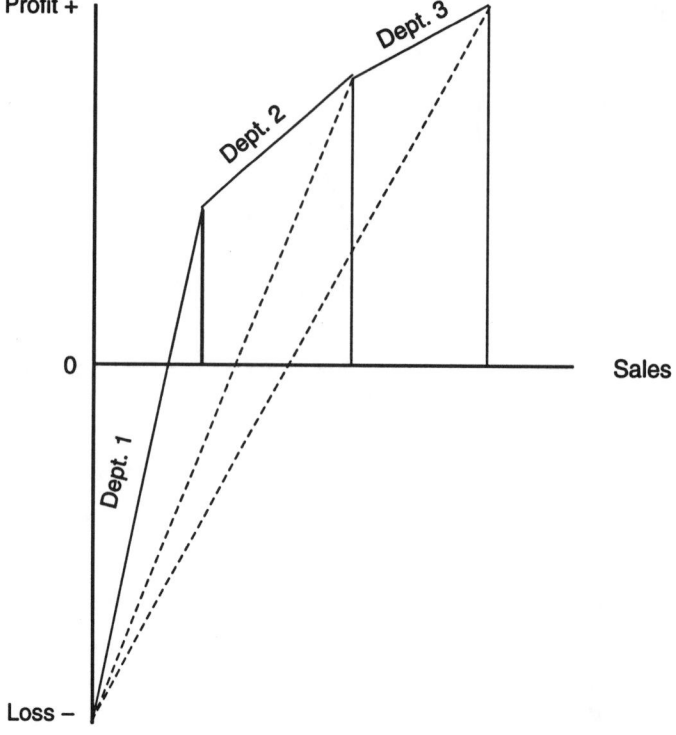

Figure 3.13   Sequential profit/volume graph

- higher levels of automation
- higher research and development
- greater advertising to achieve required volumes
- a policy of quantity discounting to maintain volume
- high gearing.

High variable costs

High variable cost businesses will tend to:

- have low levels of automation
- be direct material intensive (tending to make direct materials a high percentage of direct cost)
- find purchasing is of prime importance
- need to maintain profit margins
- have lower operational leverage.

EXERCISE

The Cumberland Hotel has three main divisions: bedrooms, restaurant/bar and conference/banqueting. During the past quarter, sales revenue was £300 000 and variable costs £190 000. Fixed costs were £65 000.

1   Calculate the P/V ratio and draw a P/V graph.

More detailed management accounting information has become available for the three divisions.

	Sales	Variable costs
Beds	£140 000	£40 000
Restaurant	£100 000	£70 000
Conference	£60 000	£80 000
Total	£300 000	£190 000

2   Calculate the individual P/V ratios and plot a cumulative line on the P/V graph. Suggest any course of action that might be taken on the basis of the information disclosed.

ANSWER

1   P/V ratio = contribution/sales × 100

= 110 000/300 000 × 100
= 36.7%

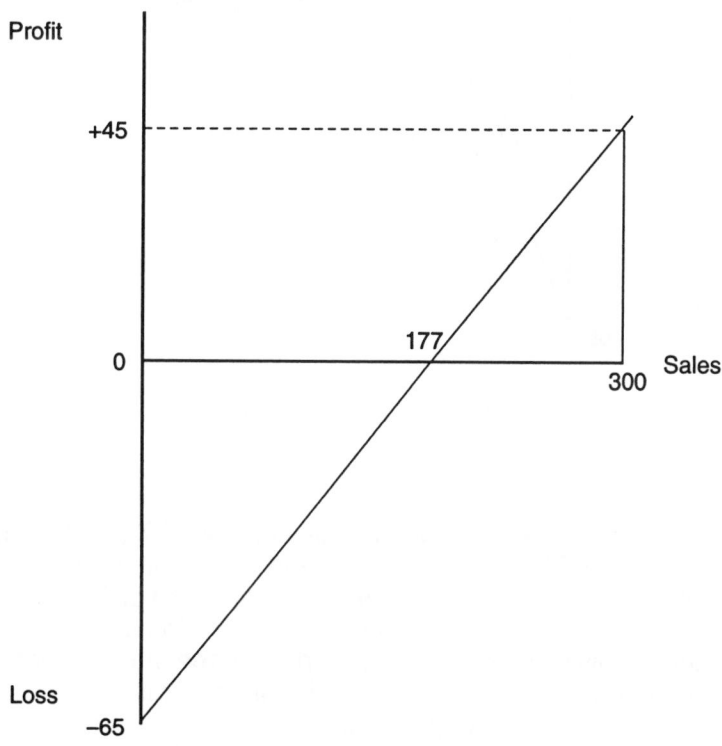

Figure 3.14   P/V graph (all figures are in £000s)

Break-even = fixed costs/P/V ratio
= 65/36.7%
=177

	Sales	Variable costs	Contribution	P/V ratio
Bedrooms	140 000	40 000	100 000	71.5
Restaurant	100 000	70 000	30 000	30
Conference	60 000	80 000	−20 000	−33.3
Total	300 000	190 000	110 000	36.7

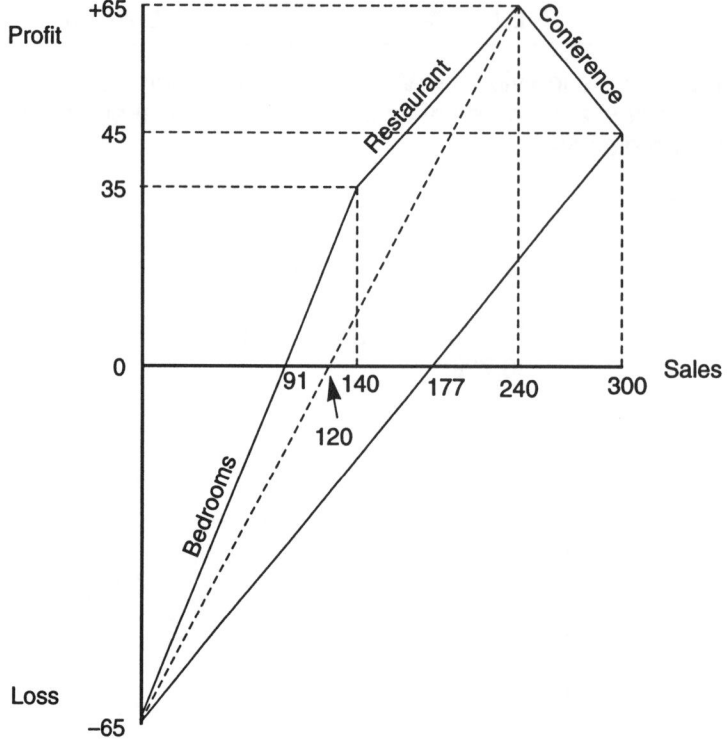

Figure 3.15   Sequential profit/volume graph

Bedrooms alone would produce sales of £140 000, profit of £35 000 and a break-even of £91 000. Bedrooms and restaurant together produce sales of £240 000, profit of £65 000 with a break-even of £120 000.

The obvious course of action would be to stop the conference and banqueting as this division does not even cover the marginal costs. This course of action may also reduce some of the fixed costs.

There will be some dependence between the three divisions and dropping conferences and banqueting may affect the other two divisions.

Some consideration should be given to increasing prices in the loss making division so the marginal costs are at least covered.

Activity based costing

In the late 1980s a book, written by Professors Johnson and Caplan and titled *Relevance Lost – The Rise and Fall of Management Accounting*, was published in the USA. The main theme of the book was that the traditional costing systems, particularly absorption costing, were no longer relevant to today's technologies.

Many companies recover their overheads on the basis of direct labour hours or direct labour cost. With advances in technology, direct labour has tended to become a smaller proportion of total costs while overheads have tended to increase. The overhead recovery rate tends to get bigger and bigger and the absorbed overhead becomes a significant proportion of the total product cost.

It is felt that, if technological advances continue at the present rate, by the turn of the century the fully automated factory will be run by one man and a dog. The man is employed to switch the machines on in the morning and off in the evening and to feed the dog. The dog is trained to bite the man if he touches anything in the intervening period.

A certain Professor Cooper in the USA first suggested the name 'activity based costing' or ABC. The purpose of ABC is to provide a more accurate identification of overheads with products. A definition of ABC is 'a method of tracing costs to products rather than allocating, apportioning and absorbing them'.

ABC is based on the concept that products do not drive costs. Instead, products give rise to activities which drive costs:

Products ――――――――――――――――――→ Costs
Products ―――――――――→ Activities ―――――――→ Costs

Examples of such cost-driving activities, in the purchasing department for example, would include receiving requisitions, contacting suppliers, getting quotations, placing orders, checking invoices and so on.

As well as providing product cost information, ABC has also proved to be useful in identifying cost reduction possibilities.

ABC is the basis of **activity based management** (ABM) which uses ABC generated data for planning, controlling and decision making.

Companies using ABC include IBM, Unipart, Norwich Union, Cummins Engines and British Airways.

ABC jargon

cost objects   products, services, customers, marketing channels.

cost pools   the sum of all the cost elements within a cost object centre is called a cost pool. Those activities driven by the same cost driver are collected in cost pools.

activity centres   stores, maintenance, distribution, administration, production, material handling, purchasing.

cost driver   the factor that drives costs in each activity cost pool, for example, the number of journeys made, the number of telephone calls, the number of parts produced, the number of requisitions, the number of orders and the number of test hours.

facility sustaining expenses   those costs that cannot be allocated to products.

Absorption compared with activity based costing

The main differences between absorption and activity based costing are shown in Figure 3.16. The following is an example of activity based costing.

The finance department's key activities are identified as invoicing customers, issuing credit notes, credit control, issuing and receiving cheques, paying wages and so on.

A cost pool is set up for each major activity and costs assigned thereto; for example, the costs of invoicing customers was £20 000 in a four-week period. The cost driver for this activity is the number of sales made, which was 10 000 items in the four weeks. The unit cost of this activity is therefore £2 per item and this cost will be assigned to each product group on the basis of the number of items sold.

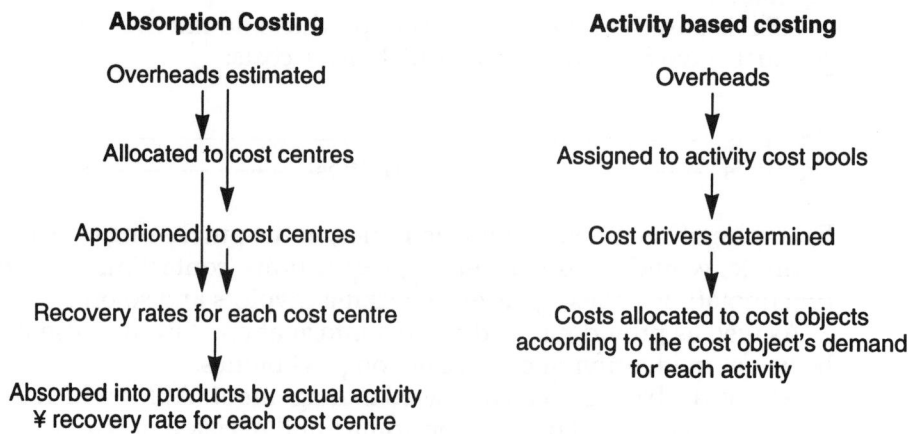

Figure 3.16   Absorption and activity based costing

EXERCISE

Zeus Optics Ltd manufactures and markets the ZSI camera. The company's trading results for the year ending 30 June 199X are as follows:

		£	£
Sales			120 000
Less	Direct material	40 000	
	Direct labour	24 000	
	Overhead	36 000	100 000
Profit			20 000

For the forthcoming year it is planned to reduce the selling price of the camera by 10 per cent which it is considered will increase sales volume by 50 per cent. Other matters affecting the forthcoming year are:

- One half, in value, of the material required will be subject to price increases of 10 per cent.
- A 5 per cent increase in the hourly wage rate will be payable to the direct labour force.
- Of the above overhead, £20 000 represents costs of a fixed nature, £10 000 represents costs which are controllable by management who plan to mount a cost reduction campaign and effect a saving of £2000, and the remaining £6000 represents costs which vary with production.

You are required to:

1 prepare a statement showing the trading result planned for the forthcoming year
2 calculate the break-even points and margins of safety for both years
3 comment briefly upon the matters which must receive management attention prior to embarking upon an expansion policy of this nature.

Note: Labour is variable in this business.

ANSWER

199X				1991	
£	£			£	£
1					
	120 000	Sales			162 000
40 000		Less: Direct material	63 000		
24 000		Direct labour	37 800		
6 000	70 000	Variable overheads	9 000		109 800
	50 000	Contribution			52 200
	30 000	Fixed overheads			28 000
	20 000	Profit			24 200
2					
	42%	P/V ratio			32%
	17%	Profit margin			15%
	£71 500	BEP on sales			£87 500
	60%	BEP as % of sales			54%
	40%	Margin of safety			46%

3   Management should consider the following:

1   Can the management cope with this expansion?
2   What will the working capital cash flow problems be?
3   Will any extra capital equipment be required?
4   Is the additional labour force available?
5   How accurate are the assumptions made?
6   Is the additional material available?
7   What will the competitors do?
8   What other permutations of price, volume and profit are there?
9   What will the return on capital employed be

- in comparison with year 1?
- in comparison with leaving things as they are?

10   Will the fixed overheads be affected by inflation?

4 Budgetary control

The first three chapters of this book have outlined the basic principles of management accounting. The remaining chapters will have a greater emphasis on how to understand and use management accounting.

This chapter will consider **control**. Control is the action taken when there is a difference between what was planned to happen and what did happen. There must therefore be a plan before control can be exercised. Control occurs when the differences between the actual performance and the planned performance move outside pre-determined tolerance limits.

Budgetary control compares 'actual' figures with 'budgeted' figures. In many cases the figure for 'actual' – be it sales or expense – may be incorrect or a best estimate. The 'actual' figure is supplied by the financial accounting system, which is not infallible. The 'actual' figures for a particular period may not be available until, perhaps, ten to fifteen days into the next period because of the multiplicity of entries or because figures have to be obtained from different locations.

The main reason businesses fail is because of lack of management control in situations such as the following:

- There is no plan or the plan is unrealistic.
- The 'actuals' are wrong, late or not available.
- No action is taken when the 'actuals' differ from the plan.

The three stages of budgetary control are:

1   planning
2   preparation
3   control.

Planning

The most important stage of the process, requiring face-to-face negotiation and communication, is planning. Policy objectives should be defined in specific terms and will vary from organisation to organisation. These should include:

- profitability – expressed as a percentage of capital employed, gross profit margins and trading profit as a percentage of sales
- solvency – expressed in terms of cash flow and a target current assets to current liability ratio
- sales growth – this should be controlled as too rapid a growth could lead to a cash shortage, a situation known as 'overtrading'
- market share
- personnel development.

Strategies should be developed stating how the objectives are to be achieved. Alternative plans will be considered and the master plan (budget) selected must give the maximum profit consistent with long-term financial stability. The assumptions behind the master budget need to be stated and could include:

- predicted inflation rates – general and specific
- percentage increases in sales and costs
- product mix
- interest rates
- exchange rates.

It is at this stage that the limiting factors (see page 42) are identified. To achieve a certain level of sales may require production capacity or skilled labour that the organisation does not have. The limiting factor that most companies face is the amount of sales that can be achieved taking into account the number of customers and the size of the competition.

Limiting factors can either be overcome by a variety of strategies or accepted in the short term.

Preparation

The process of preparation starts by deciding what the limiting factor is and budgeting this first. In most businesses this will be sales. This is probably the most difficult area to forecast but the most important to get right. The other budgets are, in the main, dependent on the sales budget, particularly the direct costs, sales and distribution costs and cash budgets.

These points should be considered when preparing the sales budget:

- price and volume per product
- target contributions per product
- past and present sales – price and volume

- competitors' prices
- market share and that of competitors – present and projected
- seasonality
- current orders
- quotes given
- advertising and marketing spend
- economic outlook
- application of the SWOT technique (strengths, weaknesses, opportunities and threats).

The sales budget will be broken down as follows:

1 by period – normally month by month
2 by product
3 by area
4 by salesperson
5 by customer.

The use of standard (expected) selling prices will speed up the budget preparation, particularly if a computer is used. Tables 4.1, 4.2 and 4.3 give examples of sales budgets broken down by product, cost and customer.

Table 4.1 Sales budget – units

Product	Price	Qtr. 1	Qtr. 2	Qtr. 3	Qtr. 4	Total
A	£6	3 000	5 000	6 000	4 000	18 000
B	£7	4 000	6 000	7 000	5 000	22 000
C	£8	5 000	7 000	8 000	3 000	23 000

Table 4.2 Sales budget – £s

Product	Qtr. 1	Qtr. 2	Qtr. 3	Qtr. 4	Total
A	18 000	30 000	36 000	24 000	108 000
B	28 000	42 000	49 000	35 000	154 000
C	40 000	56 000	64 000	24 000	184 000
Total	86 000	128 000	149 000	83 000	446 000

Table 4.3 Sales budget – customers (£s)

Customer	Qtr. 1	Qtr. 2	Qtr. 3	Qtr. 4	Total
1	15 000	40 000		16 000	71 000
2	15 000	20 000	6 400	4 000	45 400
3	16 000	10 000	18 600		44 600
4	4 000	4 000			8 000
5	3 000	5 000	30 000	6 000	44 000
6	12 000	1 000	43 000	14 000	70 000
7	1 000		12 000		13 000
8	4 000		19 000	43 000	66 000
9	3 000	20 000	20 000		43 000
10	13 000	28 000			41 000
Total	86 000	128 000	149 000	83 000	446 000

Points 1 and 2 above will form the basis for the production budget. The use of standard costs will again aid the budgeting process.

The material requirements as highlighted by the production budget will form the basis for the purchasing budget. Present and proposed stock levels will need to be taken into account. The buyer should be involved in the preparation of this budget. Such factors as price increases, discounts, credit terms, alternative materials, exchange rates, and so on must be input into the planning process.

The sales and distribution costs budget will be developed from the sales budget, whilst the administration budget can be prepared using historical data.

The capital expenditure budget will reflect proposed investments in fixed assets, such as those required to achieve the sales and production targets.

The cash budget is affected by the others and is the deciding factor in whether the plan can be achieved.

The individual budgets are brought together into the budgeted profit and loss account and budgeted balance sheet.

The three criteria for successful budgeting are:

1   Budgets must be believable.
2   Budgets must be achievable.
3   Managers must be involved in the preparation of their own budgets.

The UK subsidiary of a US corporation was told that its current level of loss was unacceptable and that its budget for the coming year was to achieve a 50 per cent reduction in the loss figure. Half-way through the following year the US company received a telex from the UK company which read 'Your target loss achieved. Await further instructions'.

This is an example of 'compelled budgeting' which is not to be recommended. 'Participative budgeting', where managers have an input into the budget preparation, is more likely to produce realistic budgets.

Budgets may fail because of:

- lack of clear communication between managers themselves and between managers and the finance department
- manipulation of the figures
- lack of understanding of the aims of the budgeting process resulting from lack of education and training
- lack of co-operation from managers who view budgeting as another vested interest of the finance department.

Flexible budgets

A flexible budget is one that is adjusted to take account of actual activity. A flexible budget compares the budgeted cost of producing, for example, 800 units with the actual cost (see Table 4.4).

Table 4.4 Flexible budget

	Original budget	Flexed budget	Actual	Variance	
Production (units)	1 000	800			
	£	£	£	£	
Direct materials	10 000	8 000	8 700	700	Adverse
Direct labour	5 000	4 000	4 600	600	Adverse
Variable overheads	1 000	800	850	50	Adverse
Fixed overhead	3 000	3 000	3 200	200	Adverse
Totals	19 000	15 800	17 350	1 550	Adverse

These variances would be analysed to see if they might have been caused by:

- price
- efficiency
- volume

and to establish if they were:

- controllable/uncontrollable.

Checklist for budget planning and preparation

- What is the timetable for the budgeting process?
- Are there any new company policies and procedures, new legislation/tax changes?
- Is there a statement of goals and objectives as set by top management?
- Are strategies agreed on how to achieve goals and objectives?
- Has base period data been selected or is zero-based budgeting* to be used?
- Have percentage increases/decreases in revenues and costs been estimated?
- Have new products, customers and distribution channels been taken into account?
- Have product mix changes and discontinued products been taken into account?
- Has the split between direct and indirect costs been agreed?
- Has the split between fixed and variable costs been agreed?
- How are overheads to be allocated – absorption, marginal or ABC?
- Has the effect on working capital and cash flow of decisions on borrowing, retention of profits and share issues been taken into account?

---

*Zero-based budgets assume no prior base period data. They are used primarily in budgeting for projects. All activities have to be justified by using cost–benefit analysis.

Spreadsheet application – budgets

The budgets in Tables 4.5–4.11 have been prepared using an IBM PC and a spreadsheet package ('As Easy As').

The company manufactures and sells three products, A, B and C, which are each made with three materials. Product A is made with materials X, Y and Z, product B with materials P, Q and R and product C with materials S, T and U. The standard material quantities and standard material prices are input into the computer as are the standard hours and the standard rates for the direct labour (Tables 4.5 and 4.6).

The sales budget is built up on a quarterly basis inserting the standard selling prices and the expected units of sale. Multiplying the standard selling prices by the expected volumes gives the budgeted sales amounts.

Any changes in the estimated figures will automatically cause the budgets to be adjusted. The projected changes in the stock figures will provide the production targets and the budgets for direct materials and direct labour.

(The purchases budget and the labour budget have not been produced on a quarterly basis in this example.)

Table 4.5 Standard cost of products A, B and C

Product	Material	Direct £/kg	Material £/kg	Cost £
A	X	0.5	2	1
	Y	1	3	3
	Z	1.5	1.5	2.25
				6.25
B	P	0.75	1	0.75
	Q	1	0.9	0.9
	R	1.25	1.2	1.5
				3.15
C	S	0.5	0.5	0.25
	T	0.6	0.6	0.36
	U	0.7	1.2	0.84
				1.45

The standard cost is the expected cost of the products.

The standard material cost is arrived at by multiplying the expected quantities of the different materials by the expected price of these materials. The expected quantities would take account of likely scrap and wastage whilst the expected material prices would be the estimated average prices to be paid in the coming year.

Table 4.6 Direct labour

Product	Std. time	Std. rate per hr.	Total £	Labour budget £s
A	0.5	6	3	51 000
B	1	6.5	6.5	149 500
C	1.5	5	7.5	157 500
				358 000

Similar remarks apply to the standard direct labour cost. The standard times would be arrived at by using time and motion and work study techniques. The standard rates would take account of any likely increases during the year.

Table 4.7 Sales budget – units

Product	Standard price	Qtr. 1	Qtr. 2	Qtr. 3	Qtr. 4	Total
A	15	3000	5000	6000	4000	18 000
B	16	4000	6000	7000	5000	22 000
C	16	5000	7000	8000	3000	23 000

The target selling prices form the basis for the sales budget. Initially the sales budget is expressed in units per product and per quarter and the computer calculates the sales budget in £s by multiplying the standard selling prices by the budgeted quantities. Changes in selling prices or budgeted quantities can be easily inserted, and the computer will immediately update all the figures.

Table 4.8 Sales budget – £s

Product	Qtr. 1	Qtr. 2	Qtr. 3	Qtr. 4	Total
A	45 000	75 000	90 000	60 000	270 000
B	64 000	96 000	112 000	80 000	352 000
C	80 000	112 000	128 000	48 000	368 000
Total	189 000	283 000	330 000	188 000	990 000

Table 4.9   Production budget – units of finished goods (O/S = opening stock, C/S = closing stock)

Product	O/S	C/S	Diffn.	Sales	Production
A	3000	2000	1000	18 000	17 000
B	8000	9000	–1000	22 000	23 000
C	4000	2000	2000	23 000	21 000
C/S in £s @ standard mfg. cost					
18 500					
86 850					
15 900					
121 250					

The production budget is calculated by taking the stock differences between the beginning and end of the year figures and adjusting the sales figures (from the sales budget) accordingly.

Table 4.10   Purchases budget

Material	O/S	C/S	Kg for production	Purchases kg	£s
X	3 000	4 000	8 500	9 500	19 000
Y	5 000	4 000	17 000	16 000	48 000
Z	7 000	9 000	25 500	27 500	41 250
P	10 000	3 000	17 250	10 250	10 250
Q	12 000	6 000	23 000	17 000	15 300
R	26 000	12 000	28 750	14 750	17 700
S	7 000	8 000	10 500	11 500	5 750
T	6 000	5 000	12 600	11 600	6 960
U	3 000	2 000	14 700	13 700	16 440
Total purchases budget					180 650

The purchases budget considers the opening and closing stocks of the various materials and calculates, from the production budget, the quantities required for production. The purchase requirement then follows and this is converted into £s by multiplying the relevant standard material price.

Table 4.11   Closing stock in £s

Material	£s
X	8 000
Y	12 000
Z	13 500
P	3 000
Q	5 400
R	14 400
S	4 000
T	3 000
U	2 400
Total	65 700

Control

Control occurs when there is a material divergence from the plan. The process of control can be subdivided into:

- reading and interpreting reports
- analysing the variances
- identifying the causes of the variances
- taking action.

Control documentation should include:

- monthly trading results
- sales, orders taken, quotes and enquiries
- aged debtor analysis
- aged creditor analysis
- stock position
- cash/overdraft situation – current and projected
- cost analysis
- ratios
- unit indicator report (financial score card).

A unit indicator report, or financial score card, is a monthly summary of the key ratios for the company. A suggested layout follows.

UNIT INDICATOR REPORT

Month . . . .   Same
                          J F M A M J J A S O N D   Mth PY*
Ratio

Return on capital
Return on sales
Gross margin
Materials as % of sales
Labour as % of sales
Overheads as % of sales
Sales/capital
Working capital as % of sales
Debtor days
Creditor days
Stock turn
Current ratio
Acid test
Gearing
Interest cover
Sales/employee
Profit/employee
Capital/employee

---

*PY = Previous year

Variances

A **variance** is the difference between budgeted and actual results. If the result gives rise to a greater profit than budgeted then it is a favourable variance. If it gives rise to a lower profit it is an unfavourable or adverse variance.

The questions that arise with material (as opposed to immaterial) variances are:

- What is the cause of the variance?
- What should be done about it?

The most likely causes of variances are:

- price changes – wage rates, material prices
- usage/efficiency – amount of material or hours worked
- overtime
- supplier changes
- sales price changes
- sales volume changes
- policies and procedure changes
- product mix
- wastage
- poor stock control
- incorrect budget
- quality changes
- machine breakdowns.

The following steps should be taken when a variance occurs:

- Summarise highlights (i.e. those variances falling outside a set tolerance – for example more than 10% different from budget).
- Analyse variances.
- State causes.
- Recommend action.
- Take action.

Summary

Figure 4.1 summarises the procedure of budgetary planning, preparation and control.

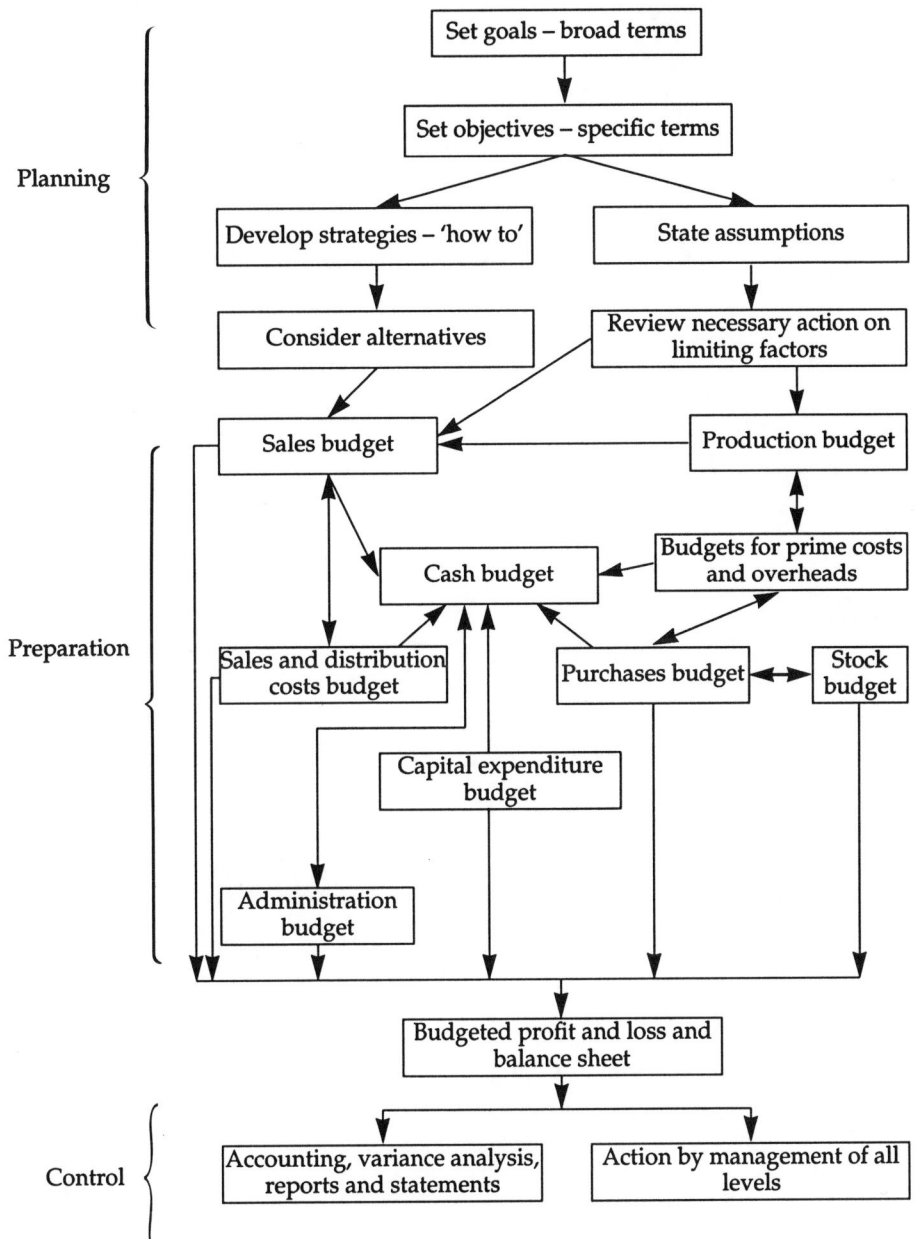

Figure 4.1   Budgetary control procedure diagram

5 Financial reports

This chapter considers the preparation and use of financial reports and graphs. The examples have been prepared on an IBM PC using a spreadsheet package ('As Easy As'). Even the smallest business is now able to produce similar presentations with the price of computer hardware and software reducing all the time.

Such presentations are useful, not only for the owners and managers of the business, but also for keeping lenders informed on the progress of the business and as a back-up for loan requests. They are also essential when preparing business plans.

The optimum amount of information should be produced – not too little and not too much. The key graphics could be reduced in size and presented on a single sheet of paper. It is important to tailor-make the reporting system to match the requirements of the 'consumers' of such information.

Remember the three cardinal points of presenting financial data (see page 2):

1 **form** – intelligible to the recipients
2 **frequency** – as and when needed
3 **accuracy** – enough for management action.

Sales reports

It is vital to track monthly sales to spot any negative trends. As well as considering sales turnover figures in terms of £s, it might be beneficial to look at the following on a monthly basis:

● enquiries received – number, value and source
● quotes tendered – number, value and potential/existing customer name
● orders received – number, value and customer names

- reasons for loss of business

    - price
    - delivery dates
    - out of stock
    - others

- reasons for gaining business from competitors

    - price
    - delivery dates
    - range of products
    - discounts

- results of advertising and marketing campaigns
- problems and complaints

    - late delivery
    - price
    - quality
    - others

- sales to individual customers this year compared to last

    - on a month by month basis
    - on a year to date basis
    - reasons for any drop in orders

- summary of comments from

    - customers
    - potential customers
    - salespeople
    - competitors
    - others.

The charts and graphs on the following pages are examples of the kind of information that should be provided in a management accounting system.

Table 5.1 shows the sales revenues from five products, comparing budget with actuals for the current month and the year to date figures. The actual sales for the same month last year and last year's year to date sales are also shown. Figure 5.1 is a graphical representation of the current month's figures taken from Table 5.1, whilst Figure 5.2 shows a pie chart illustrating the actual sales revenues for the month analysed by sales area.

Figure 5.3 plots, on a month by month basis, the actual sales per month, budgeted sales per month and the actual sales for the same month in the previous year (PY).

Table 5.1   Sales analysis

	This Month			Year to date		
Product	Budget £	Actual £	Same month last year £	Budget £	Actual £	Same month last year £
A	5 600	5 400	6 500	21 000	20 600	19 200
B	4 500	3 400	3 200	18 000	15 600	17 000
C	4 500	4 300	2 300	18 000	21 200	21 000
D	2 300	5 600	3 200	10 000	11 500	10 000
E	1 800	1 200	1 800	8 000	7 500	5 900
Total	18 700	19 900	17 000	75 000	76 400	73 100

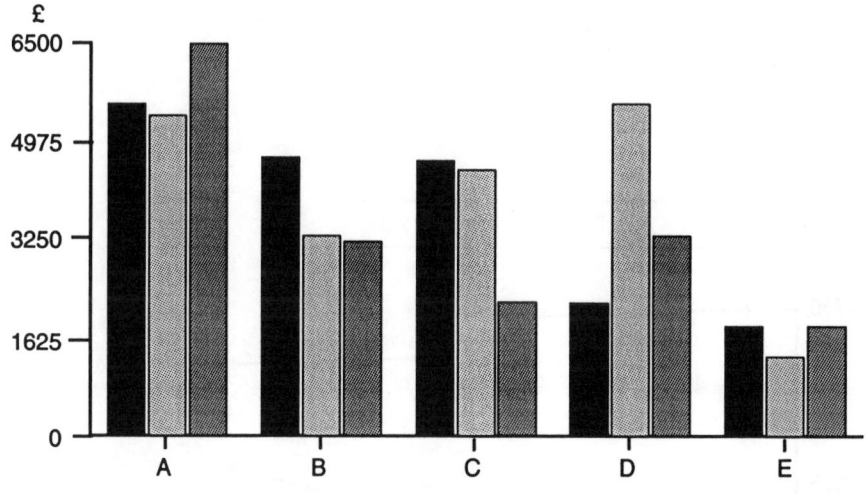

Figure 5.1   Sales analysis

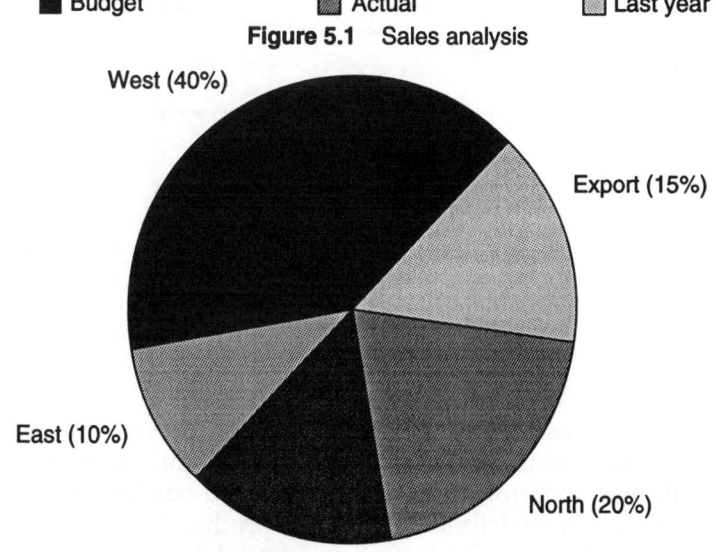

Figure 5.2   Sales by area (monthly)

Another very effective way of spotting trends is to produce a moving yearly sales figure, adding the latest month's sales and deducting the sales figure for the corresponding month last year, for example:

Month	Sales This year (£)	Sales Last year (£)
J	130	
F	140	140
M	120	120
A	130	130
M	180	180
J	260	260
J	140	140
A	140	140
S	140	140
O	140	140
N	110	110
D	100	100
J		120
Total	1 730	1 720

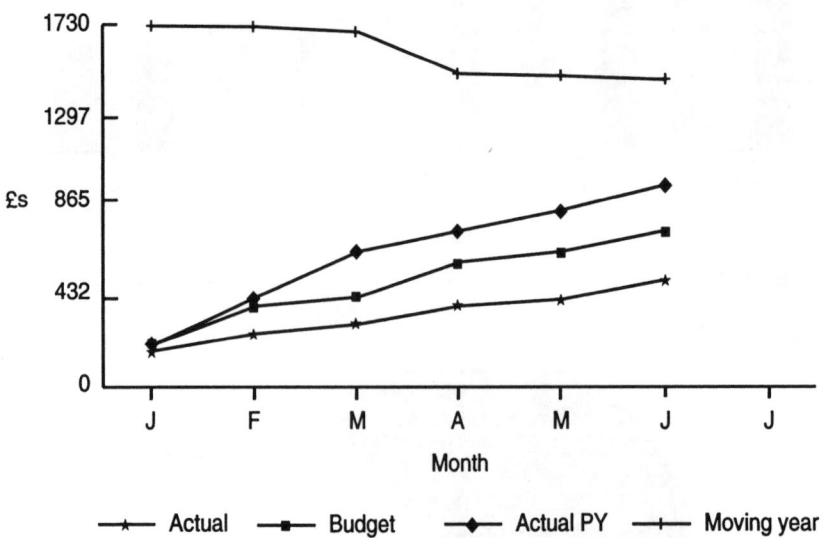

Figure 5.3   Year to date sales analysis

Figure 5.4 shows sales, contribution and profit on a month by month basis. This presentation is useful in spotting trends. Comparisons with budgets and with previous year's figures would be illuminating.

Table 5.2 is a contribution analysis, product by product, showing sales and contributions, both planned and actual, for the current month and the year to date. The percentage of contribution to sales for each product could

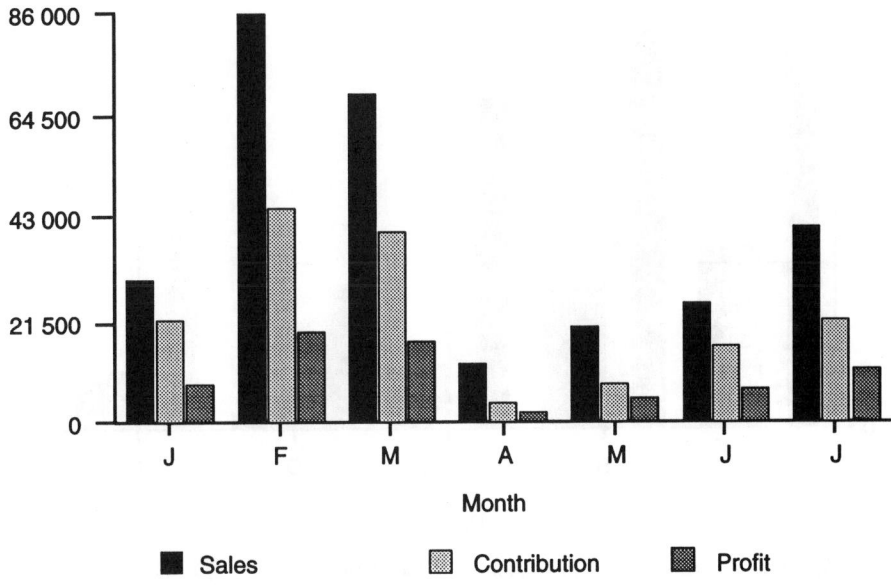

Figure 5.4   Sales, contribution and profit

Table 5.2   Contribution analysis

Product	This month Sales budget £	Sales actual £	Cont. budget £	Cont. actual £	Year to date Sales budget £	Sales actual £	Cont. budget £	Cont. actual £
A	19 800	21 000	9 800	9 500	56 000	58 000	28 000	29 000
B	21 000	19 800	8 000	7 300	63 000	61 000	20 000	18 000
C	17 600	14 300	3 400	3 200	54 000	49 000	10 000	7 000
D	7 600	8 700	1 200	900	21 000	23 000	3 000	4 000
E	12 000	10 000	3 000	2 500	38 000	35 000	9 000	8 000
Total	78 000	73 800	25 400	23 400	232 000	226 000	70 000	66 000

also be calculated. Figure 5.5 is a graphical representation of the monthly figures in Table 5.2.

Figure 5.6 shows, on a month by month basis, assets employed and working capital. These figures would be extracted from the monthly balance sheet.

In Table 5.3 the overheads are shown as percentages of total overheads. On the operating statement they will probably be shown as a percentage of sales. The trends in both sets of percentages are important. The variable overheads will tend to increase with increases in sales, whilst the fixed overheads will tend to increase over time.

The capital expenditure on five projects is illustrated in Table 5.4 which shows the estimated total expenditure and expenditure to date.

Figure 5.7 gives a graphical representation of the capital expenditure each month, whilst Figure 5.8 shows the cumulative interest cost on a month by month basis.

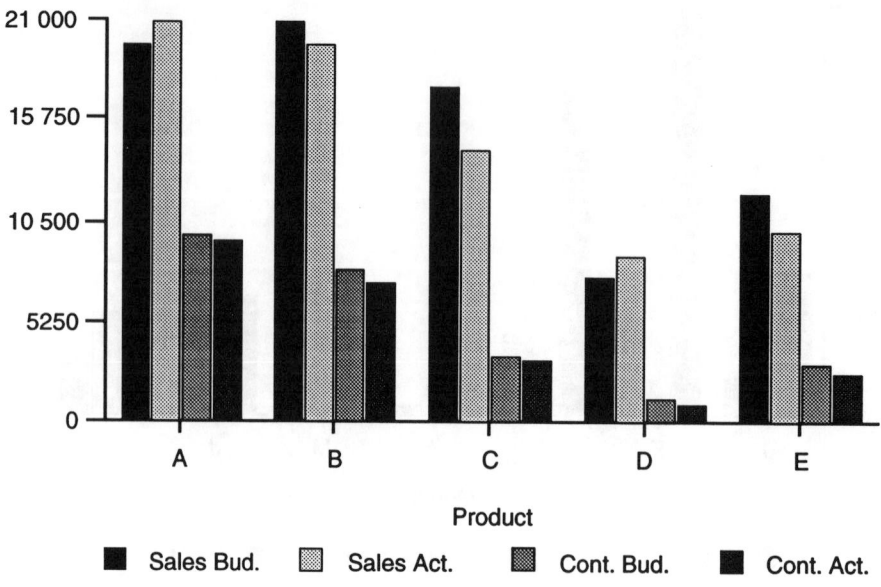

Figure 5.5   Contribution analysis

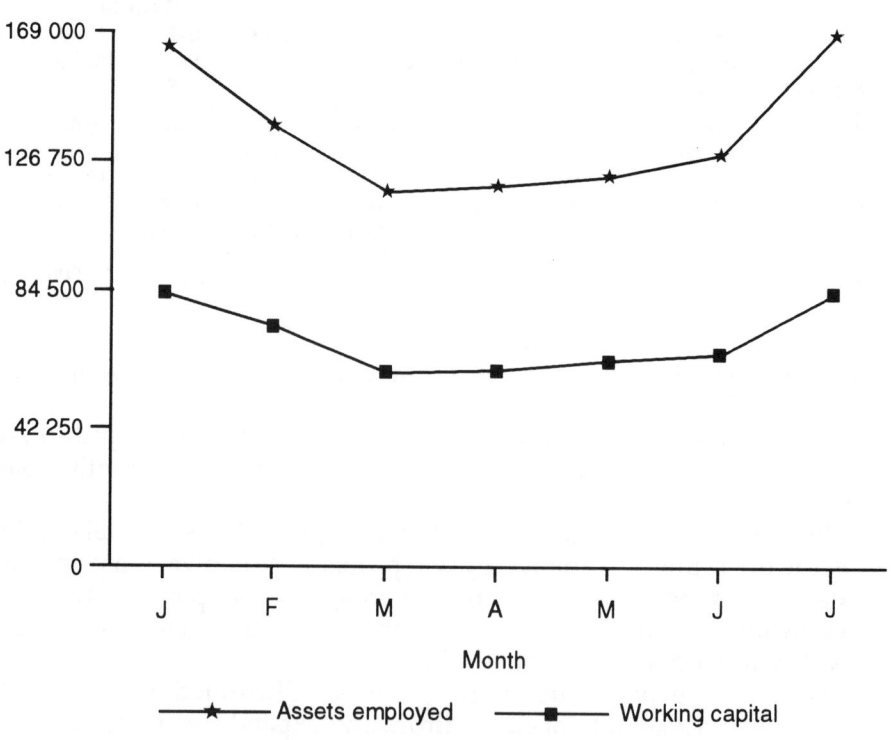

Figure 5.6   Assets employed

Table 5.3 Overhead analysis

| | This month | | | | Year to date | | | |
| | Actual | | Budget | | Actual | | Budget | |
	£	%	£	%	£	%	£	%
Manufacturing								
Administration								
Sales and distrib.								
Total overheads		100%		100%		100%		100%

Table 5.4 Capital expenditure analysis (monthly)

Project	Original budget £	Revised budget £	Expenditure to date £	Comments	Expected completion date
R	56 000	68 000	43 000		
S	23 000	25 000	19 000		
T	18 000	17 000	12 000		
U	58 000	52 000	43 000		
V	87 000	90 000	49 000		
Total	242 000	252 000	166 000		

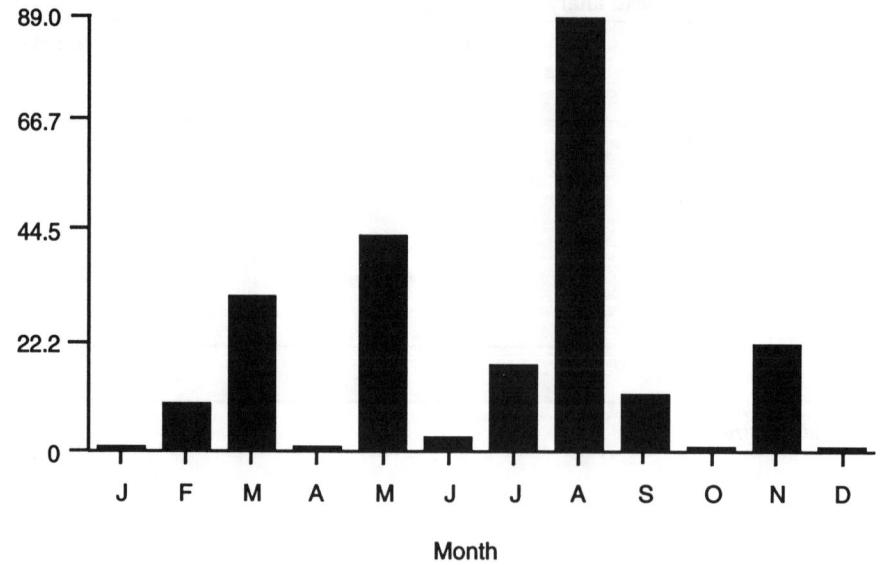

Figure 5.7   Capital investment

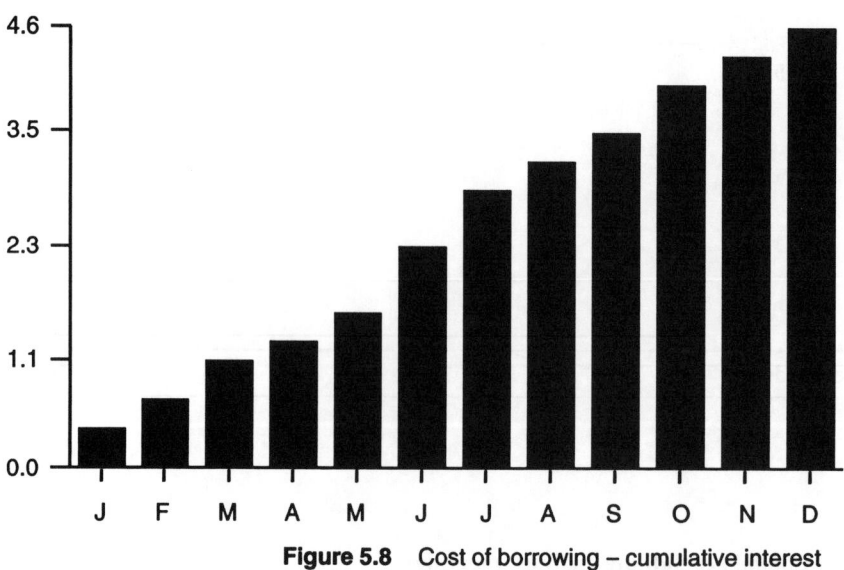

Figure 5.8   Cost of borrowing – cumulative interest

These tables and figures should serve as a guide to the presentation of management accounting information. Each organisation should, of course, tailor its presentations to suit its own individual requirements.

Stock control

The objective of stock control is to achieve the right balance between having too much money tied up in stock and having too little stock with a high probability of 'stock-out' situations.

The consequences of having excess stock are:

- interest cost on money tied up
- cash flow problems
- increased obsolescence, wastage and pilferage
- increased handling costs
- increased storage space
- increased environmental and safety problems
- increased insurance cost.

The consequences of having very low stock are:

- increased ordering costs
- higher prices for rush deliveries
- lost production
- loss of business or customer goodwill
- less able to react if problems at suppliers
- less able to cope with seasonal fluctuations
- more vulnerable to commodity price rises, currency fluctuations or impending price increases by the supplier.

Pareto or ABC analysis

At the end of the last century, Pareto (1848–1923) analysed the distribution of income and wealth in Italy and discovered that 80 per cent of the income and wealth was in the hands of 20 per cent of the population. One doubts if the figures would be any different today.

This uneven distribution of value can be seen in a variety of business situations:

- 80 per cent of a company's sales will tend to go to 20 per cent of its customers.
- 20 per cent of a company's products will produce 80 per cent of its profits.
- In the stores, 80 per cent of the value is contained in 20 per cent of the volume.

Stock can be classified into A, B and C type stock depending on its value. For example, the most valuable items may make up 80 per cent of the value but only make up 20 per cent of the volume. These would be the A category items. The next 30 per cent in volume representing 15 per cent of the value might be the B category items, whilst the remaining 50 per cent of items representing 5 per cent of the value would be the C category items.

A category items would be subject to closer control than B and C category items.

An illustration of ABC analysis

Firstly, for all items in stock, the estimated usage for a period is multiplied by the estimated unit price to give the estimated total purchase price.

Table 5.5   Stock listing

Item	Est. usage	Est. price £	Est. total purchase price £
A	50 000	1.20	60 000
B	10 000	0.80	8 000
C	1 000	1.12	1 120
D	5 000	5.00	25 000
E	100 000	0.10	10 000
F	8 000	4.00	32 000
etc.			
Total	200 000		1 000 000

Next list the items in descending order of unit price.

Table 5.6   ABC analysis of stock listing

No.	Item	Est. usage	Est. price £	Est. total £	Cumulative £
1	D	5 000	5.00	25 000	25 000
2	M	2 000	4.80	9 600	34 600
3	F	8 000	4.00	32 000	66 600
etc.					
100		100 000	0.10	10 000	1 000 000
Total		200 000		1 000 000	

Now plot the cumulative totals against the item numbers, as demonstrated in Figure 5.9. In Figure 5.9 the first 20 items account for 50 per cent of the total value, the next 30 items represent 30 per cent of the total and the remaining 50 items represent 20 per cent of the total.

Managing debtors

After stock, the other key area of investment is the money owed by customers. These customers are called 'debtors'; in the States they are called 'accounts receivables'.

Credit management is concerned with reducing the *time* debtors take to pay as well as the *amount* outstanding. A balance must be struck between control and goodwill. Poor credit control means less profit, poor cash flow and increased risk of bad debts. Too strict an imposition of credit terms may mean losing business to competitors.

Credit management is concerned with:

- establishing creditworthiness
- monitoring the accounts
- chasing up the bad payers.

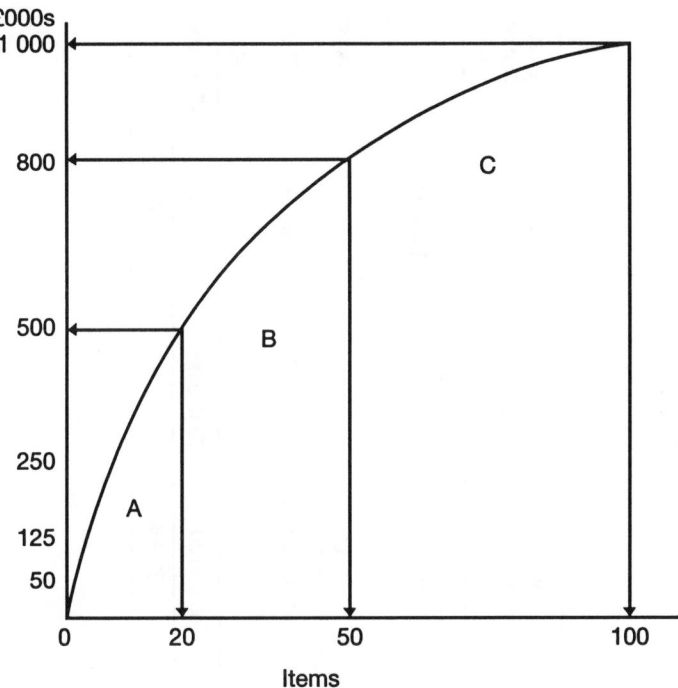

Figure 5.9   Stock distribution chart

Table 5.7   Days sales outstanding

	£	No. of Days
Sales ledger balance at end December	210 000	
Less December sales	100 000	30
	110 000	
Less November sales	80 000	30
	30 000	15*
Less October sales	60 000	
	(30 000)	

*30 000/60 000 × 30 days = 15 days

The monitoring of accounts is the province of management accounting. Information provided by the management accounting system includes:

- calculation of days sales outstanding (DSO – see Table 5.7) using the backing out method
- aged analysis of debtors (see Table 5.8)
- days sales represented by debtors (see Figure 5.10)
- monthly debtors report (see Table 5.9)
- cash collected as a percentage of cash collectable (see Table 5.10).

Table 5.7 illustrates the use of the backing out method. From the sales ledger

Table 5.8 Aged analysis of debtors

Customer	Total debt £	Current month £	'C'	Total overdue £	30–60 days £	60–90 days £	90–120 days £	over 120 days £
A1 Ltd	560.00	200.000		360.00	210.00			
B2 Ltd	2 100.00			2 100.00	500.00	150.00	1 600.00	
C3 Ltd	420.00	420.00						
D4 Ltd	21.00	21.00						
E5 Ltd	56.00			56.00	28.00			28.00
F6 Ltd	28.00			28.00	28.00			
G7 Ltd	3 475.00	2 000.00		1 475.00	1 000.00	200.00	200.00	75.00
etc.								
Z26 Ltd	963.00						363.00	600.00
Totals	180 000.00	75 000.00		105 00.00	60 000.00	23 000.00	7 000.00	15 000.00
	100%	41.7%		58.3%	33.3%	12.8%	3.9%	8.3%

Notes: Have a 'comments' column to record details of payment chasing.
Modify to own requirements.
'c' = category of debtor (see 'Pareto Analysis', page 85).

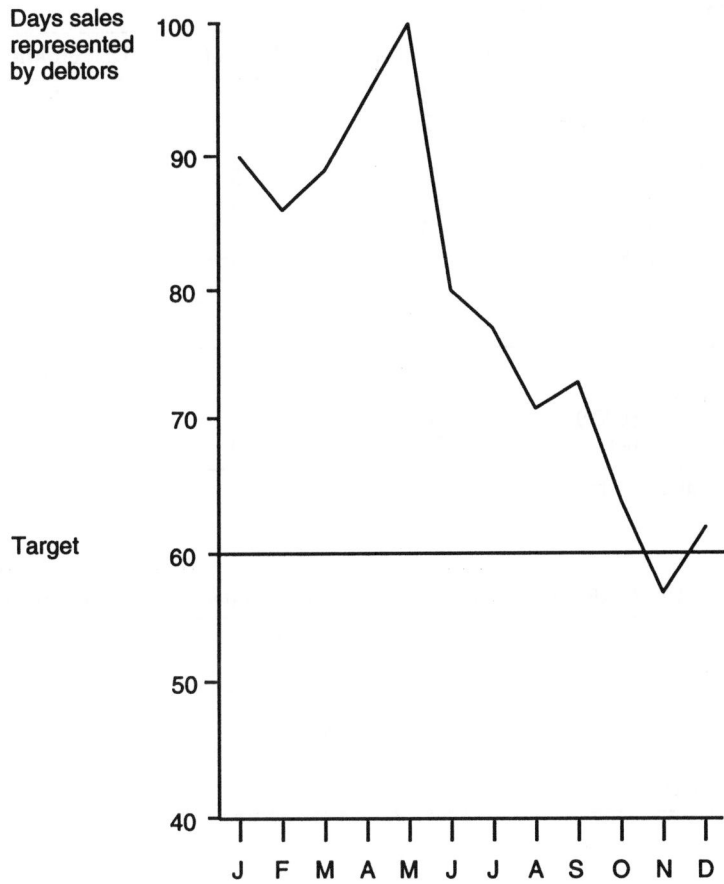

Figure 5.10   Days sales represented by debtors

balance for a particular month, that month's sales and previous months' sales are deducted until the balance is eliminated. Each month's sales figure that is deducted is equivalent to 30 days. In this example the sales ledger balance at the end of December amounted to £210 000 and the average days sales outstanding figure (DSO) was 75 days.

Each month's DSO can be plotted on a graph, as in Figure 5.10, to show the credit control performance.

Table 5.8 is a suggested layout for an aged debtor analysis. The customers are listed, perhaps in alphabetical order or in descending order of size. The total debt for each customer is then shown and this is then further analysed as to the amount not yet overdue, the amount overdue and how long the overdue amounts have been outstanding. Each column is totalled and expressed as a percentage of the total debt. The perentages should be compared with budget and with previous months' figures. The credit controller should concentrate on the oldest amounts outstanding, and should spend more time on the larger amounts.

Table 5.9   Monthly debtors report

	This month	Budget	Last month	Last year
DSO	63	60	65	66
Overdues (% of SL)*	52	50	48	46
Overdues (%s)				
1–30 days	76	75	74	70
31–60 days	20	25	18	25
61–90 days	3		6	3
91–120 days	1		2	1
121 + days				1
	100%	100%	100%	100%
Disputes (% of SL)*	4	4	4.3	4.2
Sales (£000s)	280	300	260	220
Collections (£000s)	220	230	210	200
Debtors (£000s)	550	620	610	600

*SL = sales ledger

Table 5.10   Cash collected as percentage of cash collectable for sales made in August

	Cash collected %	Unpaid %
August	5	95
September	20	75
October	65	10
November	10	0

Table 5.11   Percentage of cash unpaid

	J	F	M	A	M	J	J	A	S	O	N	D
Same month	96	92	94	91	90	96	97	95	95	94	91	90
Prev. month	80	81	77	74	72	70	76	77	75	70	69	68
2 months ago	15	13	13	14	12	10	9	9	8	10	12	7

Table 5.9 is a monthly debtors report which summarises the credit control performance. Figures are provided for the current month, both actual and planned, the previous month and the same month last year. A graphical presentation would also be useful.

Table 5.10 tracks the collection of each month's sales by converting the sales figure into 100 per cent and showing the percentage of that month's sales that remain outstanding at the end of each month. For example, if August sales are 100 per cent and 5 per cent has been collected by the end of August then 95 per cent remains collectable. If, in September, 20 per cent of the August sales are collected then, at the end of September, 75 per cent of the August sales remain unpaid. In October 65 per cent is collected and the remaining 5 per cent collected in November. The collection of each month's sales can be tracked by examining the left to right diagonal pattern in Table 5.11.

EXERCISE – PARETO ANALYSIS ON A SALES LEDGER

1   Re-list all the balances in the 'total overdue' column in descending order of value i.e. start with the largest.
2   Beside each balance on the list, record the cumulative value.
3   Give each balance a number i.e. number 1 for the largest, and so on.
4   Plot a graph from the information shown in the table that has been created. In practice, select a few items to plot on your graph rather than plotting every item.

ANSWER

Table 5.12   Debtor distribution chart

Value of overdue balances £	Cumulative value of balances £	Balance number
11 000	11 000	1
10 000	21 000	2
8 000	29 000	3
6 000	35 000	4
4 000	39 000	5
1 000	40 000	6
etc.	etc.	etc.
etc.	etc.	etc.
601	70 000	20
592	70 592	21
etc.	etc.	etc.
etc.	etc.	etc.
104	94 000	50
99	94 099	51
etc.	etc.	etc.
etc.	etc.	etc.
3	99 997	93
2	99 999	99
1	100 000	100

Pareto analysis in the control of debtors

If Pareto analysis is adopted in cash collection, it enables different techniques and timetables to be applied to different categories of debt. Pareto analysis allows priorities to be set using clear cut criteria.

Although it is a common sense principle, the full value of Pareto analysis is not always appreciated. If it is viewed as the main criterion for credit control activity, the value of categorisation can be clearly seen:

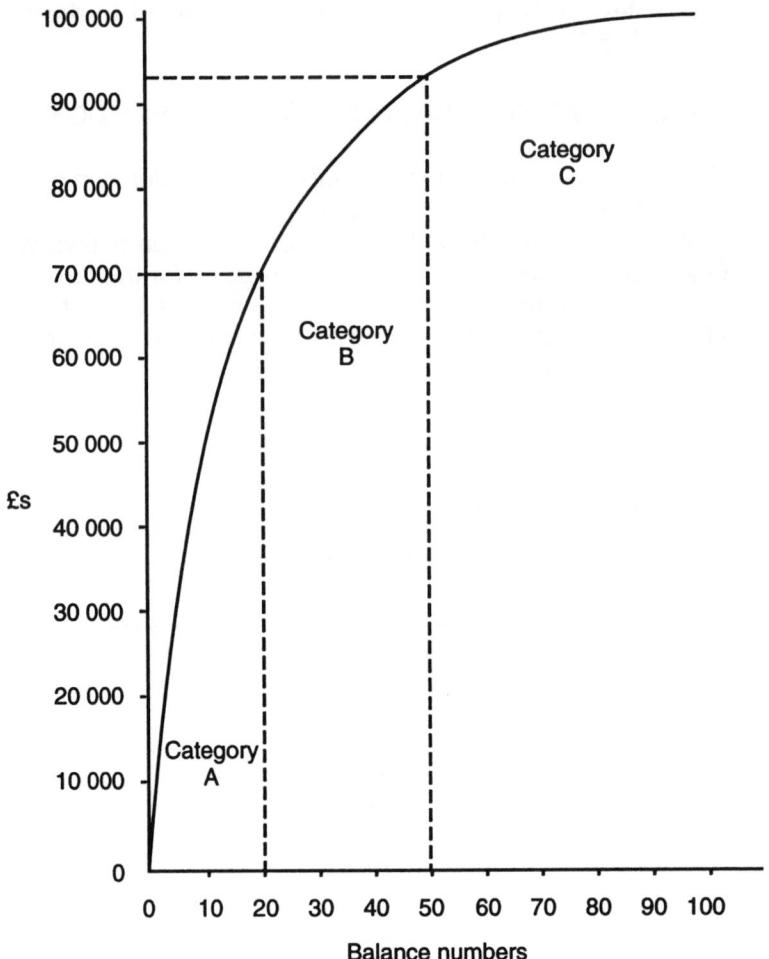

Figure 5.11   Debtor distribution graph

- by reducing the number of bad debts – a bad debt sustained in the category A area may well be disastrous; a bad debt in the category C area, whilst being undesirable, is hardly likely to have the same effect on a company's financial stability.
- by improving liquidity – efforts fed into the category C area may produce large reductions in the average age of debt outstanding in that area, but the effect on liquidity will be very small; a small reduction in the average debt age in the category A section will produce a substantial improvement in liquidity.
- by increasing profit – similar to the effect on liquidity, substantial efforts applied to category C debts will have little effect on profit.

Whilst it could be a recipe for disaster to take a Pareto approach too far (in other words to ignore category C debts altogether), it is necessary to

Table 5.13   Credit control performance chart – aged debtor analysis

Customer no.	Customer name	Total overdue £	Current month £	30–60 days £	61–90 days £	91–120 days £	120+ days £
123		10 700	7 500	3 200			
345		11 800	6 500	2 100	3 200		
456		2 369	1 900	230		239	
789		14 700	6 700	4 300	1 600	1 200	900
543		31 000	13 000	7 000	6 000	3 000	2 000
Totals (1)		70 569	35 600	16 830	10 800	4 439	2 900
%		100	50.4	23.8	15.3	6.3	4.1
Sales for each month		(2)	35 600	28 000	100 000	80 000	100 000
(1) as % of (2)		(3)	100.0	60.1	10.8	5.5	2.9
% which should be O/S		(4)	100.0	80.0	10.0	2.5	2.5
(3) as % of (4)		(5)	100.0	75.1	108.0	221.9	116.0
Total line (5)		621					

Notes:
Line (1) is the totals from the current month's aged debtor analysis.
Line (2) shows the sales for the particular months. The 120 day + total would be the average of the previous three months.
Line (3) calculates Line (1) totals as a percentage of line (2).
Line (4) are the percentages which *should* be outstanding.
Line (5) calculates line (3) percentages as a percent of line (4) percentages.
If the total of the line (5) figures is exactly 500 then the target performance has been achieved. Less than 500 means a better than target performance, over 500 a worse than target performance.

have the priorities in mind when operating any system. Otherwise there is a danger that the limited time available will be spread too thinly over all the outstanding debts leading to a failure to achieve worthwhile results.

The aged debtor analysis can be used to produce the credit control performance chart which is a superior way of evaluating the performance compared to the calculation of the DSO. The chart tracks performance on a month by month basis and discloses the trend. The numbers in the chart have no meaning in themselves. A figure of 500 means target performance has been achieved; a figure below 500 means actual performance exceeds the target; and above 500 means target performance has not been achieved.

In Table 5.13 the total of line 5 is 621 which is a fair performance compared to target (500).

Figure 5.12, which depicts performance trends in terms of index numbers, shows that performance was good in January and February but that the trend was negative from March to May. Performance then improved, with August's performance better than target. Since then, the trend has been disappointing.

Managing creditors

Creditors, or accounts payable as they are known in the States, are those suppliers who still have to be paid.

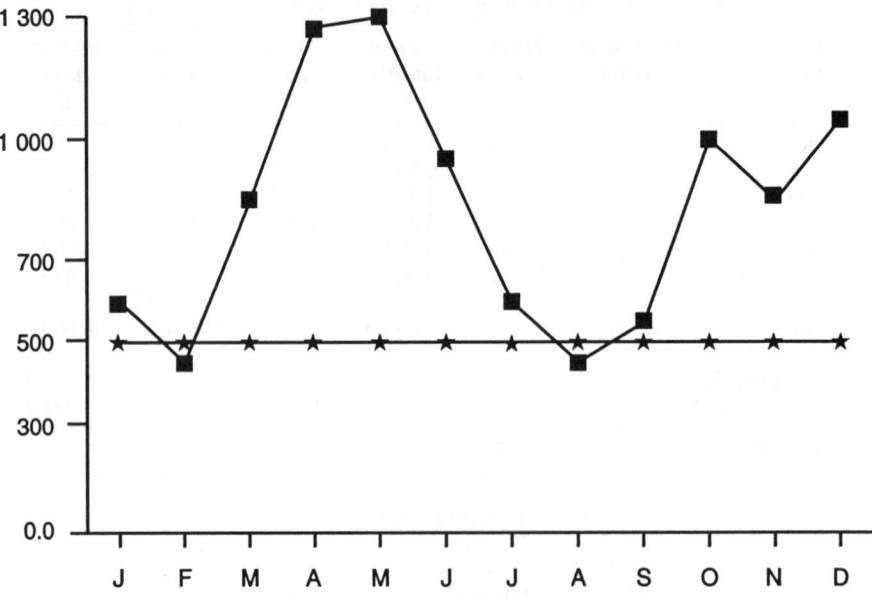

Figure 5.12   Credit control performance chart

The policy towards creditors should be the opposite of that applied to debtors. Profit and cash flow will be improved if payment to suppliers is delayed and the amount of credit taken is maximised. After all, credit is the most attractive form of finance – it's free! However, the goodwill aspect must not be overlooked. Delaying payment will in the long run lead to higher prices as suppliers seek to recover their interest costs.

Other disadvantages of extended delay are:

- problems of supply, after-sales service
- damage to reputation from bad credit references
- cost of legal action by suppliers.

From a credit management point of view, it is important to produce an aged creditor analysis on exactly the same lines as the aged debtor analysis (see Table 5.14).

This analysis highlights those creditors who have not been paid for some time and are likely to be getting impatient. It is also useful as a check on the validity of payment demands from suppliers and is a prime source of the payment figures in the cash budget. A comments column may be included to state why particular payments have not been made. For example, in Table 5.14 there are amounts outstanding for more than 120 days. Why?

A graphical representation of debtors and creditors, as illustrated by Figure 5.13, helps to compare debtors with creditors each month and also discloses the trends in these amounts.

Table 5.14 Aged creditor analysis

Supplier no.	Supplier name	Total overdue	Current month	30–60 days	61–90 days	91–120 days	120+ days
123		12 900	7 600	5 400			
234		19 000	6 000	6 100	6 900		
456		5 009	1 900	2 870		239	
789		14 700	6 700	4 300	1 600	1 200	900
543		21 129	3 000	7 690	5 439	3 000	2 000
675		5 610	3 420	2 190			
Totals (1)		78 348	28 520	28 550	13 939	4 439	2 900
%		100	36.4	36.4	17.8	5.7	3.7

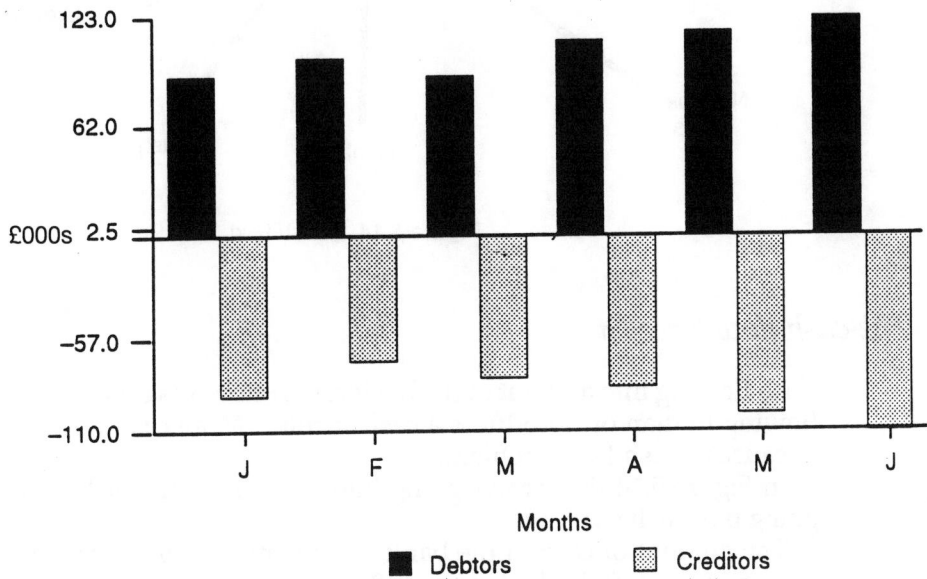

Figure 5.13 Debtors and creditors

Cash control

The control of cash is just as important as the control of stock or the control of debtors. Cash must be made to work for the company by:

- investing it
- using it to get better discounts
- ploughing it back into the working capital circle
- reducing borrowings
- updating capital equipment.

Organisations should consider banking every day rather than once a week.

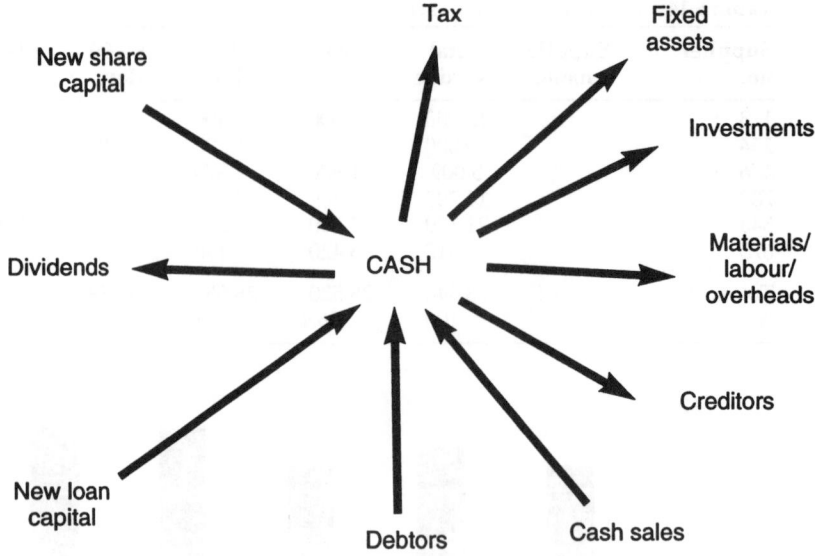

Figure 5.14   Cash flow

The cash flow forecast

Cash flowing into and out of the business is known as **cash flow**. More cash flowing in than out produces a cash surplus. More cash flowing out than in causes a cash flow problem.

In Figure 5.14 the arrows going into cash represent cash inflows, those going out, cash outflows.

The amount of cash in the bank, or the amount of overdraft needed, is shown in the cash budget, or cash flow forecast. Sometimes a surplus will be forecast which should be invested to earn interest. At other times an overdraft might be needed which will mean additional interest to pay. The cash flow forecast shows the ability of a business to fulfil its plans.

If a company runs out of cash, other people, such as creditors, bankers and employees, will start to make the decisions.

The layout of a cash flow forecast is shown in Table 5.15.

The following points should be remembered when preparing a cash flow forecast for the bank:

- the more detail the better
- the 'Actual' column should be completed
- the final figures should be in black.

Cash flow – summary

- There is no attempt to differentiate between capital and revenue. All that needs to be considered is **cash**.

Table 5.15 Cash flow forecast

	January		February	
	Budget £	Actual £	Budget £	Actual £
Receipts				
Cash sales				
Debtor payments				
Sale of fixed assets				
New share capital				
New loans				
Total cash in	35		45	
Payments				
Cash payments				
Payments to creditors				
Wages and salaries				
Rent				
Rates				
Heat and light				
etc.				
Interest				
Dividends				
Loan repayments				
VAT				
Purchase of fixed assets				
Total cash out	25		30	
Surplus/(deficit)	10		15	
Opening balance	3		13	
Closing balance	13		28	

- The closing balance one month becomes the opening balance the next.
- The 'Actual' column should be completed as soon after the event as possible.
- The actuals should be used to re-plan the cash for the coming twelve months – continuous budgeting.
- The managers 'closest to cash' should be involved in the budgeting process. They are:
  - the sales manager
  - the credit controller
  - the works manager
  - the buyer
  - the personnel manager
  - the company secretary
  - the accountant.
- The cash flow forecast is the most important financial statement of all. It is not subject to judgement as is the profit and loss account. It is not subject to 'window dressing' as is the balance sheet. It is not prepared

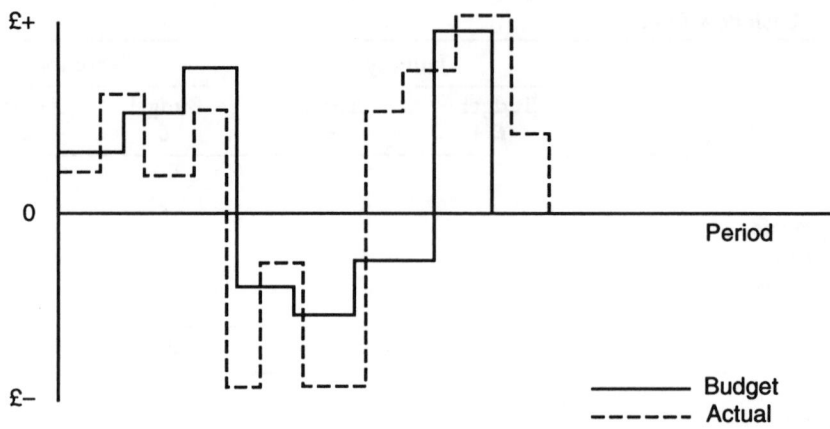

Figure 5.15   Graphical presentation of bank balances

according to accountants' conventions. The only thing that matters is the cash coming in and the cash going out.

Cash or overdraft positions can be plotted as in Figure 5.15.

6 Ratio analysis

Ratio analysis is a very useful way of evaluating the strengths and weaknesses of an organisation, since it is concerned with the relationships between figures rather than the figures themselves.

There are four stages in ratio analysis:

1 understanding how money moves in a business
2 organising the data ⎫
3 measuring the data ⎬ using a spreadsheet package
4 interpreting the data. ⎭

Key ratios

The key ratios for the particular business should be selected and calculated on a monthly basis. Comparisons should be made with:

- previous months
- other businesses in the same industry
- industry averages
- budgeted ratios
- results for different divisions, departments or product groups.

Key ratios include:

Return on capital employed

$$\frac{\text{trading profit}}{\text{capital}} \; \%$$ indicates effectiveness of capital utilisation

The UK average figure is around 18 per cent. The trend should be rising and generally speaking the higher the figure the more profitable the company.

The capital figure should include any revaluation of the fixed assets but should exclude intangibles such as goodwill, trade marks, patents and brand names. Opinions differ as to the correct definition of 'capital', but most analysts take the total of the fixed assets and the working capital. Investment income should be excluded from the profit figure whilst investments (other than trade investments) should be excluded from the capital figure.

The following return on capital percentages may be useful as a guide to how well a company is performing.

0–10%	Poor
10–15%	Not bad
15–20%	Average
20–25%	Good
25–30%	Excellent
30%+%	Amazing

Return on sales

$$\frac{\text{trading profit}}{\text{sales}} \%\quad \text{indicates profit margin}$$

This ratio shows how much profit in pence is generated from every pound of turnover. The figure should be compared with previous years, with the company's competitors and with the average for the industry. Companies selling low value items in high volume for cash, for example supermarkets, cash and carries and so on, would have relatively low profit margins, say 5–7 per cent, whilst organisations selling high value items on credit and with low stock turns would have higher profit margins (they would need to have higher margins to provide for the delay in payment and the cost of carrying stock).

It is not necessarily true that the trend in this figure should always be rising. A company with a lower profit margin than its competitors might increase its market share at their expense. Selling more at lower margins might increase the return on capital employed figure.

Asset velocity

$$\frac{\text{sales}}{\text{capital}} \%\quad \text{indicates sales force's effectiveness}$$

The asset velocity ratio shows the amount of sales in pounds for every pound of invested capital. The definition of capital must be the same as in the return on capital employed figure.

These three ratios are connected as follows:

profit margin $\times$ asset velocity = return on capital employed

For example,

$5\% \times 6 = 30\%$ 1994
$4\% \times 8 = 32\%$ 1995

Here a discount warehouse has undercut the supermarket competition by charging less (lower profit margin), but its greater asset velocity has generated a greater return on investment.

Gross profit margin

$$\frac{\text{gross profit}}{\text{sales}} \ \% \qquad \text{indicates pricing policy}$$

The gross profit margin is an important figure, particularly for retailers and wholesalers. It indicates the pricing policy of the organisation. It is a key figure in the calculation of break-even (see below). Trends are very important, as are comparisons with other similar companies. A drop in the figure means a higher break-even point and a lower margin of safety.

Break-even

$$\frac{\text{fixed costs}}{\text{gross profit margin}} \qquad \text{indicates sales needed before a profit is made}$$

This shows, in percentage terms, how much sales can fall from their present level before the company starts to make a loss. As a general rule the figure should not fall below 30 per cent.

Operational leverage

$$\frac{\text{fixed costs}}{\text{total costs}} \ \%$$

The greater the amount of operational leverage, the higher the break-even point will be and the lower the margin of safety.

Working capital control

$$\frac{\text{working capital}}{\text{sales}} \ \% \qquad \text{indicates relationship between 'luggage' and sales}$$

The trend in this figure should be gradually downwards because a company should be reducing its stock and debtor levels (and increasing its creditors) so that profit and cash flow are improved whilst risks are reduced. Too rapid a drop in the figure could indicate overtrading, whilst an increase might indicate a lack of working capital control.

Alternatively, the ratio of sales/working capital could be calculated and in this case we would look for gradual increases.

Fixed asset turnover

sales/fixed assets

This ratio shows how effective the sales force is in producing sales compared with the capital employed in fixed assets.

Debtor days

$$\frac{debtors}{sales} \times 365 \qquad \text{indicates effectiveness of credit control}$$

The trend in the DSO (days sales outstanding) figure should be reducing and should be lower than competitors' figures and lower than the average for that industry. The UK average figure is 80 days.

Creditor days

$$\frac{creditors}{purchases} \times 365 \qquad \text{indicates effectiveness of credit management}$$

The creditor days should, if possible, be longer than the debtor days. If not, the company may have a cash flow problem.

Stock turn

$$\frac{stock}{cost\ of\ sales} \times 365 \qquad \text{indicates time taken to sell stock}$$

For companies selling low value items in quantity for cash the time taken to shift stock will be low. For organisations selling high value items on credit the time taken to convert raw materials into sales will tend to be much greater.

An alternative calculation is sales (cost)/stocks. This figure should be increasing.

Cash cycle analysis

stock turn + debtor days – creditor days

This shows the time taken to turn stock into cash less the time taken to pay suppliers. The trend should be reducing.

Current ratio

$$\frac{\text{current assets}}{\text{current liabilities}} \quad \text{indicates ability to pay short-term debts}$$

Current assets represent the money in the till or coming into the till over the next few weeks or months, whilst current liabilities represent the bills which need to be paid.

The trend is important here. The figure should not be too high (over-weight!) nor too low (anorexic!).

The average for engineering/manufacturing companies is about 1.3:1, whilst supermarkets and cash and carries often have a current ratio of less than 1:1 which would not necessarily be dangerous for this type of organisation.

Acid test

$$\frac{\begin{array}{c}\text{current assets}\\ \text{(excl. stock)}\end{array}}{\text{current liabilities}} \quad \text{indicates more stringent test of liquidity}$$

This ratio indicates the ability of the firm to pay its short-term liabilities without having to rely on its slow moving stock. The figure should ideally be 1:1.

Stock should be included if it is rapidly converted into cash, for example stock in a supermarket.

Gearing

$$\frac{\text{loans}}{\text{shareholders' funds}} \% \quad \text{indicates use of debt to finance firm}$$

Loans include overdrafts and all capital that has to be serviced by payments of interest.

The trends are important. A rising trend might indicate a company trying to borrow its way out of trouble. Much depends on the industry as to what the figure should be, supermarkets normally having low gearing whilst property companies would normally have high gearing. The UK average is around 40 per cent.

Interest cover

$$\frac{\text{trading profit}}{\text{interest}} \quad \text{indicates ability to service debt}$$

The minimum figure should be 3.

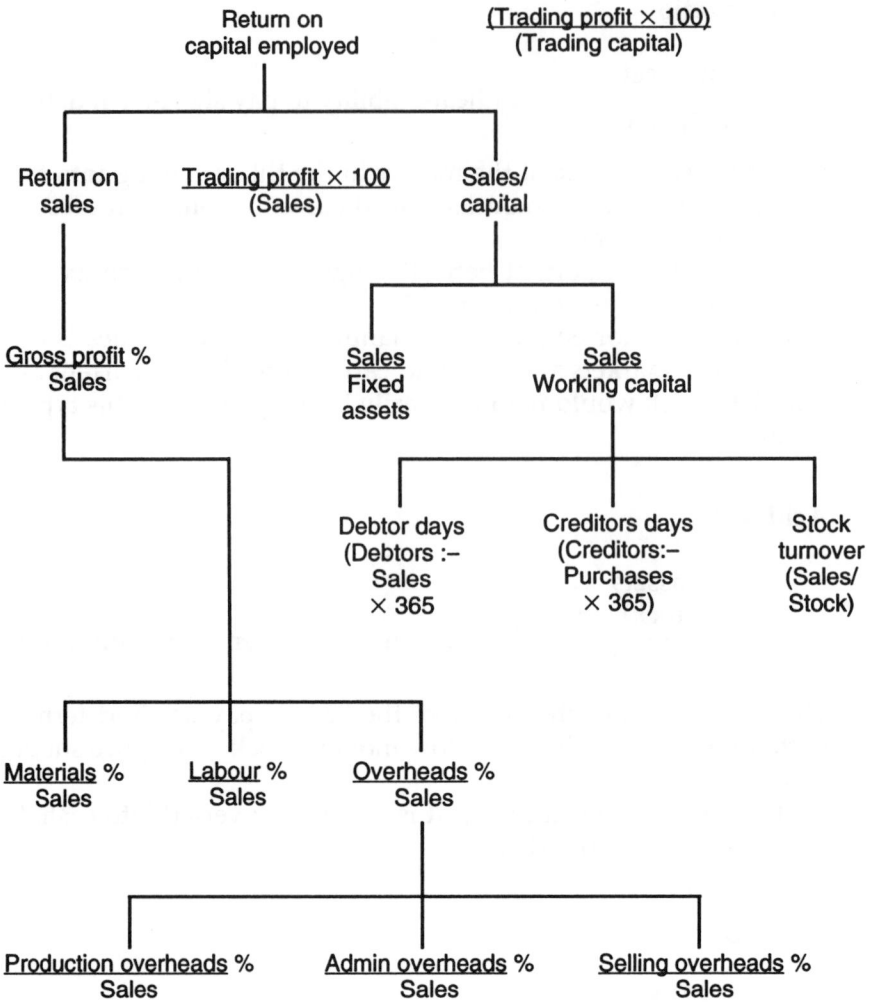

Figure 6.1   Pyramid of ratios

Debt capacity

$$\frac{\text{total debt}}{\text{net cash flow}}$$ indicates ability to repay debt

Net cash flow is defined as retained profit for the financial year plus the depreciation. The depreciation is added back because it is a non-cash expense. The total debt is compared with this figure to see how long it would take the current net cash flow to repay the current debt. This should be less than the average age of the debt. The figure should be reducing.

Working worth

$$\frac{\text{working capital} + \text{net worth}}{2}$$

This should be a positive figure; the larger the figure the larger the credit limit should be. A negative figure indicates possible insolvency and the credit limit should be zero.

Financial strength

$$\text{current ratio} + \text{acid test} - \frac{\text{current liabilities}}{\text{net worth}} - \frac{\text{long-term liabilities}}{\text{net worth}}$$

> 1	excellent
1 to –2	good
–2 to –5	reasonable
<–5	poor

Other useful ratios are shown on the financial score card (see p. 73).

Many of the above ratios are useful in the budgeting process itself. By fixing target ratios, it is possible to arrive at budgeted overhead figures (usually expressed as a percentage of sales) and budgeted figures for debtors, creditors and stock.

Many of the ratios are linked together on the Pyramid of Ratios (see Figure 6.1). This was first developed by Dupont Corporation as a way of setting targets for departments within the organisation. Actual ratios were compared with budgeted ratios on a month by month basis.

Ratio analysis can be used in management accounts and in assessing the strengths and weaknesses of a company on a yearly basis.

The use of Z scores in risk assessment

Z scoring was first devised in 1968 by Professor Edward Altman of New York University using a technique he called 'discriminant analysis'. By analysing the accounts of hundreds of companies he devised a formula for predicting corporate collapse. His formula is:

$$Z = 1.2X1 + 1.4X2 + 3.3X3 + 0.6X4 + X5$$

where

X1 = working capital/total assets
X2 = retained earnings/total assets
X3 = trading profit/total assets
X4 = market value of equity/debt
X5 = sales/total assets

A figure of less than 1.81 indicates a company is in trouble whilst 2.7+ suggests failure is unlikely.

In 1983 Altman produced a revised formula for those companies not quoted on a stock exchange:

$$Z = .717X1 + .847X3 + 3.107X3 .42X4 + .995X5$$

(X4 uses the book value rather than the market value of the equity.)

The cut-off score is now 1.23.

In 1972 Roman Lis developed the following formula for use in the UK:

$$Z = 0.063X1 + .092X2 + .057X3 + .001X4$$

where

X1 = working capital/total assets
X2 = trading profit/total assets
X3 = retained earnings/total assets
X4 = net worth/debt

Here the crucial cut-off figure is 0.037.

Taffler proposed the following formula in 1977:

$$Z = 0.53X1 + 0.13X2 + 0.18X3 + 0.16X4$$

where

X1 = trading profit/current liabilities
X2 = current assets/total liabilities
X3 = current liabilities/total assets
X4 = sales/total assets

Above 0.3 means good long-term survival prospects, below 0.2 means insolvency is likely.

To take Maxwell Communications as an example, the Z scores for the years 1989–1991, using the Taffler formula show:

1989	.37
1990	.24
1991	.22

In themselves, they do not confirm insolvency but they do indicate a worrying trend.

Another method for predicting insolvency was produced by John Argenti. He calls his method the A score. Argenti realised that most failing companies go through three distinct phases – defects, mistakes and symptoms. Points are given for each factor in each phase and a final A score is calculated.

Table 6.1 The A score method of predicting insolvency

Defects	Your score	Argentis' score
Autocratic Chief Executive		8
Chairman also Chief Executive		4
Passive directors		2
Unbalanced board		
(skill & knowledge)		2
Finance director weak		2
No management depth		
(lack of professional managers below board		
level)		1
Accounting defects:		
No budgetary control		3
No cash flow forecasts		3
No costing system		3
Little response to change		
(products, processes, markets,		
employee practices etc.)		15
Maximum possible score		43
Pass mark		10

If score more than 10, management defective and may make a fatal mistake.

Mistakes		
Gearing too high		15
Overtrading		15
The big project		
(project failure would jeopardize the company)		15
Maximum possible score		45
Pass mark		15

If cumulative score is 25+ at this stage, company is running at some risk.

Symptoms		
Financial signs deteriorate		4
Creative accounting being used		4
Non-financial signs		
(declining quality, morale, market share)		4
Terminal signs		
(writs, rumours and resignations)		3
Maximum possible score		12
Total possible A score		100
Pass mark		25
Most non-failing companies		5–18
Marks & Spencer		4
Companies in trouble		35–70

If total score is more than 25, company may fail within 5 years. The higher the score the fewer the years.

You may like to score for your own company using Table 6.1. You can either score the number of points suggested by Argenti or zero – no intermediate scores are allowed. The higher the score the worse the situation.

Ernst & Whinney (now Ernst & Young) have produced the following checklist for predicting which companies will fail. (This is obviously a bit tongue in cheek but there is more than a grain of truth in some of them.)

- directors drive Rolls Royces with personalised number plates
- fountain in reception areas
- flag-pole outside factory
- unqualified/elderly accountant
- Queen's award for industry – UK
- audit partner grew up with the company
- new offices recently opened by Prime Minister
- 'Hi-Tec' included in company name
- annual report shows chairman getting out of helicopter
- company has recently opened an office in China
- products are market leaders
- contented workforce – strike free.

In conclusion, I give you my list – the Skone or easy method for predicting insolvency.

- Is the company less than five years old?
- Is the company in a cyclical industry?
- Are the current liabilities more than the current assets?
- Is the gearing more than 100 per cent?
- Have sales increased by more than 50 per cent p.a. over the last four years?
- Are the reserves negative and more than the share capital?
- Has the company moved or is it about to move?
- Is the company using 'creative accounting'?
- Has gearing significantly increased since last year?
- Has the company recently had new bankers, new auditors, new directors?
- Is the Chairman also the Managing Director?
- Is short-term capital more than long-term capital?
- Are reports and accounts lavish or of non-standard size?

If the answer is 'yes' to more than five of these questions, be careful! If the answer is 'yes' to more than eight of these questions . . . you have been warned!

Ratio analysis using a computerised spreadsheet

The following analysis, in Tables 6.2–6.7, illustrates the application of a computerised package, FINAL ANALYSIS, developed by the author and a colleague.

The profit and loss and balance sheet figure for Polly Peck International over a four-year period have been inserted into the relevant sections of the package and the computer has done the rest. The program will produce all the relevant ratios together with Z scores and financial strength indices. In addition, a cash flow statement is produced showing the cash inflows and outflows for the period.

The package can be used for analysing annual figures or used in monthly management accounts by including moving annual figures for the profit and loss account and month-end figures for the balance sheet. There is also a graphics facility for charting the ratios and the growth or shrinkage in the key variables such as sales, profit and capital.

All figures in the following tables are in £000s.

Table 6.2   Profit and loss accounts

Company>>		Polly Peck International			
Month/Year >>		12/89	12/88	8/87	8/86
Number of Weeks >>		52	70	52	52
1) PROFIT AND LOSS STATEMENT					
Sales Turnover	[1]	1,162,300	967,100	380,846	273.717
Cost of Sales	[2]	N/A	N/A	N/A	N/A
Gross Profit		N/A	N/A	N/A	N/A
Operating Expenses	[3]	-946,625	-781,080	-275,535	-189,640
Operating Profit		215,675	186,020	105,311	84,077
Other Income/Provisions	[5]	1,325	-1,320	2,315	465
Profit on Ordinary Activities					
Before Interest and Tax		217,000	184,700	107,626	84,542
Interest Payable	[PL]	-55,600	-40,600	-21,400	-14,137
Profit Before Tax		161,400	144,100	86,226	70,405
Taxation	[PL]	-22,800	-24,500	-16,577	-9,107
Profit After Tax		138,600	119,600	69,649	61,298
Minority Interests	[PL]	-900	-1,700	-621	-75
Extraordinary Items	[6]	0	-900	408	0
Profit for Financial Year		137,700	117,000	69,436	61,223
Appropriations	[PL]	0	0	0	0
Dividends	[PL]	-49,300	-26,100	-11,891	-7,410
Retained Profit for Year		88,400	90,900	57,545	53,813
Number of Employees	[7]	17,220	13,631	5,294	3,456
Employee Costs	[7]	-97,700	-83,600	-19,200	-9,431
Depreciation Charge	[8]	-28,700	-24,400	-6,750	-4,581

Table 6.3   Balance sheets

Company>>		Polly Peck	International		
Month/Year >>		12/89	12/88	8/87	8/86
Number of Weeks >>		52	70	52	52

2)   BALANCE SHEET (Net Version)

		12/89	12/88	8/87	8/86
Fixed Assets (written-down value)					
- Intangible	[B]	284,500	0	0	0
- Tangible	[A]	1,015,800	514,800	221,195	157,861
- Intermediate	[B]	69,400	4,800	1,256	3,928
- Total:		1,369,700	519,600	222,451	161,789
Current Assets					
- Stocks	[C]	246,500	128,100	68,393	35,756
- Debtors	[C]	443,700	196,600	154,420	110,068
- Other	[C]	265,200	130,700	24,967	21,096
Total Current Assets		955,400	455,400	247,780	166,920
Creditors - Amounts falling due within one year:					
- Loans/Overdrafts	[E]	387,500	84,500	42,741	37,939
- Creditors	[E]	219,100	130,700	53,367	24,327
- Other	[E]	117,100	61,200	40,372	37,868
Total Current Liabilities		723,700	276,400	136,480	100,134
Net Current Assets/Liabilities		231,700	179,000	111,300	66,786
Total Assets less Current Liabilities		1,601,400	698,600	333,751	228,575
Less: Creditors - Amounts falling due after more than one year:					
- Long-Term Loans	[E]	-712,000	-287,460	-125,552	-61,634
- Minority Interests	[E]	-4,700	-4,140	-1,080	-78
- Other L-Term Liabilities	[E]	-41,000	-20,800	-9,886	-2,940
Net Assets/Liabilities		843,700	386,200	197,233	163,923
Capital and Reserves:					
- Called-up Capital	[D]	38,500	25,100	15,627	12,170
- Reserves	[D]	805,200	361,100	181,606	151,753
Shareholders' Funds		843,700	386,200	197,233	163,923

Table 6.4 Statements of cash flow

Company>>	Polly Peck International			
Month/Year >>	12/89	12/88	8/87	8/86
Number of Weeks >>	52	70	52	52
5) CASH FLOW STATEMENT				
5.1 – Net Cash Inflows/(Outflows) from Operating Activities				
– Profit B.I.T.	215,675	186,020	105,311	84,077
– add back Depreciation	28,700	24,400	6,750	4,581
– Other Op. Income/Prov'ns	20	30	50	60
– Prof/Loss ex Aquis'ns	1,250	-1,300	2,200	250
– Changes in Non-Cash Circulating Funds:				
– (Inc)/Dec in Stocks	-118,400	-59,707	-32,637	-6,726
– (Inc)/Dec in Dbtrs.	-247,100	-42,180	-44,352	-222,985
– Inc/(Dec) in Creds	122,800	76,029	19,593	19,997
Net Op. Inflow/(Outflow)	2,945	183,292	56,915	79,254
5.2 – Returns on Investments, and Servicing of Finance				
– Interest Received	10	15	20	20
– Interest Paid	-55,600	-40,600	-21,400	-14,137
– Dividends Paid	-26,100	-11,891	-7,410	-5,575
– Minority Interests	-340	1,360	381	31
Net Total:	-79,085	132,176	28,506	59,593
5.3 – Tax Paid	-24,500	-16,577	-9,107	-10,679
5.4 – Investing Activities: (Net Payments to Acquire/Receipts from Sale of:				
– Intangible F. Assets	-284,500	0	0	0
– Tangible F. Assets	-529,700	-318,005	-70,084	-68,417
– Intermediate Assets	-64,600	-3,544	2,672	-2,842
– Prof/Loss Sale of Ass.	45	-65	45	135
– Extraordinary Items	0	-900	408	0
– Appropriations	0	0	0	0
5.5 – Net Cash Inflow/(Outflow) before Financing:	-982,340	-206,915	-47,560	-22,210
5.6 – Financing:				
– Ord. Share Capital	369,100	98,067	-24,235	1,349
– Long-Term Loans/Liabs	444,740	172,822	70,864	22,389
S-Term Loans/O'drafts	303,000	41,759	4,802	14,232
5.7 – Net Incr/(Decr) in Cash and Cash Equivalents:	134,500	105,733	3,871	15,760
– Opening Balance	130,700	24,967	21,096	5,336
– Closing Balance	265,200	130,700	24,967	21,096

Table 6.5   Operational performance ratios

Company>>		Polly Peck International			
Month/Year >>		12/89	12/88	8/87	8/86
Number of Weeks >>		52	70	52	52
8) OPERATIONAL PERFORMANCE RATIOS					
8.1 – Annual Trends	[■]	(% of Previous Year)			
– Sales Turnover	[■]	161.8	188.6	139.1	133.2
– Profit B.I.T.	[■]	158.2	127.5	127.3	126.9
– Capital Employed	[■]	264.8	181.2	146.0	151.5
8.2 – Cumulative Trends	[■]	(% of Year 1)			
– Sales Turnover	[■]	565.5	349.6	185.3	133.2
– Profit B.I.T.	[■]	325.7	206.0	161.6	126.9
– Capital Employed	[■]	1061.1	400.7	221.1	151.5
8.3 – Key Ratio Pyramid	[■]				
P.B.I.T./T.Assets (%)	[■]	9.3	16.2	22.9	25.7
= P.B.I.T./Sales (%)	[■]	18.7	19.1	28.3	30.9
X Sales/T.Assets (X)	[■]	0.50	0.85	0.81	0.83
8.4 – Expense Analysis					
(P & L Items expressed as % of Sales Turnover)					
Sales Turnover	[■]	100.0	100.0	100.0	100.0
– Cost of Sales	[■]	N/A	N/A	N/A	N/A
	[■]				
= Gross Profit Margin	[■]	N/A	N/A	N/A	N/A
– Operating Expenses	[■]	−81.4	−80.8	−72.3	−69.3
– Other Inc./Prov'ns	[■]	0.1	−0.1	0.6	0.2
	[■]				
= Net Margin (PBIT)	[■]	18.7	19.1	28.3	30.9
– Interest Charges	[■]	−4.8	−4.2	−5.6	−5.2
– Tax	[■]	−2.0	−2.5	−4.4	−3.3
– Dividends	[■]	−4.2	−2.7	−3.1	−2.7
– Other	[■]	−0.1	−0.3	−0.1	−0.0
	[■]				
= Retained Profit	[■]	7.6	9.4	15.1	19.7
8.5 – Turnover Ratios	[■]	(Turnover/Assets)			
– Tangible F. Assets (X)	[■]	1.07	1.62	1.71	1.69
– Working Capital	[■]	5.02	4.45	3.42	4.10
– Net Assets	[■]	0.73	1.19	1.14	1.20
– Stocks	[■]	4.72	6.37	5.57	7.66
– Debtors	[■]	2.62	3.87	2.47	2.49
8.6 – 'Day Ratios'	[■]	(Variable X 365/denominator)			
– Stock (to C of S)	[■]	N/A	N/A	N/A	N/A
(to Turnover)	[■]	77	57	66	48
– Debtors (to Turnover	[■]	139	94	148	147
– Cred'rs (Purch's)	[■]	84	74	70	49
8.7 – Employee Ratios	[■]	(Variable/Employee Costs)			
– Av. Remuneration (£)	[■]	5,674	6,133	3,627	2,729
– Sales (£'000)	[■]	11.90	11.57	19.84	29.02
– Profit (B.I.T.) ''	[■]	2.22	2.21	5.61	8.96
– Capital Employed ''	[■]	16.39	9.74	17.38	24.24
– Gross Added Value					
(Productivity Ratio)	[■]	3.51	4.71	6.96	10.45

Table 6.6   Financial performance ratios

Company>>		Polly Peck International			
Month/Year >>		12/89	12/88	8/87	8/86
Number of Weeks >>		52	70	52	52
9) FINANCIAL PERFORMANCE RATIOS					
9.1 - Investment Ratios [■]					
- Return on Capital Employed					
(PBIT./Cap.Emp) (%) [■]		13.6	22.7	32.2	37.0
- Return on Equity					
(P.A.T./S.Funds) (%) [■]		16.4	26.3	35.3	37.4
9.2 - Gearing Ratios [■]					
- Capital Gearing (Total Debt					
/Ca. Employed) (%) [■]		68.7	52.8	50.4	43.6
- Equity Gearing (Shareholders' Funds					
/Total Liabs) (%) [■]		36.3	39.9	41.9	49.9
- Debt Ratio (Total Debt					
/Net Worth) (%) [■]		196.6	94.7	85.3	60.7
9.3 - 'Cover Ratios' [■]					
- Interest (Profit Before Interest and Tax					
/Interest Chgs) (x) [■]		3.90	4.55	5.03	5.98
- Dividends (Profit for Financial Year					
/Dividends) (x) [■]		2.79	4.48	5.84	8.26
9.4 - Liquidity Ratios [■]					
- Current Ratio (Current Assets					
/C. Liabs) (x) [■]		1.32	1.67	1.82	1.67
- Acid Test (or 'Quick') Ratio (Liquid Assets					
/C. Liabs) (x) [■]		0.98	1.20	1.31	1.31
- Debt Capacity (External Liabilities					
/Cash Flow) (x) [■]		8.90	4.83	3.58	2.50
- Margin of Safety ((Sales - Breakeven)					
/Sales x 100) (%) [■]		N/A	N/A	N/A	N/A
9.5 - Financial Strength Assessment					
(>1 = Excellent: 1 to -2 = Good: -2 to -5 = Reasonable: <-5 = Poor					
Current Ratio		1.32	1.67	1.82	1.67
+ Acid Test Ratio		0.98	1.20	1.31	1.31
- C. Liabs/S. Funds		-0.86	-0.71	-0.69	-0.61
- Total Debt/S. Funds		-1.30	-0.95	-0.85	-0.61
	[■]				
= Total Strength		0.14	1.22	1.58	1.76
	[■]				
9.6 - Cash Cycle Analysis					
Stock Days		77	57	66	48
+ Debtor Days		139	94	148	147
- Creditor Days		-84	-74	-70	-49
= Net Efficiency (Days) [■]		133	77	144	146

Table 6.7   Insolvency prediction scores

Company>>	Polly Peck International			
Month/Year >>	12/89	12/88	8/87	8/86
Number of Weeks >>	52	70	52	52

10)   SOLVENCY PREDICTION RESEARCH RATIOS

10.1 – W. H. Beaver (1966) [■] (Each measure is an independent indicator)

	12/89	12/88	8/87	8/86
– Group 1 – Cash Flow (Cash Flow /Total Debt) [■]	0.15	0.33	0.45	0.66
– Group 2 – Net Income (Profit After Tax /Total Assets) [■]	0.06	0.11	0.15	0.19
– Group 3 – Debt (Total Debt /Total Assets) [■]	−0.47	−0.38	−0.36	−0.30
– Group 4 – Liquidity (Working Capital /Total Assets) [■]	0.10	0.19	0.24	0.20

10.2 – E. Altman (1983)

10.2.1 – Individual ratios

	12/89	12/88	8/87	8/86
– 'x1' – Liquidity (Working Capital /Total Assets)	0.10	0.19	0.24	0.20
– 'x2' – Profitability (Retained Earnings /Total Assets)	0.35	0.37	0.39	0.46
– 'x3' – Gearing (P.B.I.T. /Total Assets)	0.09	0.16	0.23	0.26
– 'x4' – Solvency (Shareholders' Funds /Total Debt)	0.77	1.06	1.17	1.65
– 'x5' – Activity (Sales /Total Assets)	0.50	0.85	0.81	0.83

10.2.2 – Weighted ratios and Z-Score (Cut-Off Point = 1.23)

	12/89	12/88	8/87	8/86
– Liquidity (x1) x 0.717	0.07	0.14	0.17	0.15
– Profitability (x2) x 0.847	0.29	0.32	0.33	0.39
– Gearing (x3) x 3.107	0.29	0.50	0.71	0.80
– Solvency (x4) x 0.420	0.32	0.44	0.49	0.69
– Activity (x5) x 0.998 [■]	0.50	0.85	0.81	0.83
– Altman Z-Score [■]	1.48	2.25	2.51	2.86

10.3 – Lis

10.3.1 – Individual ratios

	12/89	12/88	8/87	8/86
– 'x1' – Liquidity (Working Capital /Operating Assets)	0.11	0.19	0.24	0.20
– 'x2' – Profitability ((P.B.I.T. + Depreciation) /Operating Assets)	0.09	0.14	0.21	0.24
– 'x3' – Retained Earnings (Reserves /Operating Assets)	0.39	0.37	0.39	0.46
– 'x4' – Gearing (Shareholders' Funds /Total Debt)	0.77	1.06	1.17	1.65

10.3.2 – Weighted ratios and Z-Score (Cut-Off Point = 0.037)

	12/89	12/88	8/87	8/86
– Liquidity (x1) x 0.063	0.007	0.012	0.015	0.013
– Profitability (x2) x 0.092	0.008	0.013	0.020	0.022
– Ret. Earnings (x3) x 0.057	0.022	0.021	0.022	0.026
– Gearing (x4) x 0.001 [■]	0.001	0.001	0.001	0.002
– Total Lis-Score [■]	0.039	0.047	0.058	0.062

7 Pricing

This chapter considers the purpose of pricing policy and the different methods used to arrive at a selling price. It illustrates, by sensitivity analysis, the effect of price rises and reductions on the bottom line. Finally, some pricing strategies are described.

Pricing policy

The aim of pricing policy is to arrive at selling prices that produce volumes of sales that maximise profit. Profit is a function of price, volume, cost and product mix.

Other factors to be considered in developing a pricing policy are:

- advertising and marketing
- packaging
- after-sales service
- delivery times
- stability of suppliers
- credit terms.

Pricing methods

Cost-plus

The cost-plus method of pricing adds a percentage mark-up to cost to arrive at the selling price, for example:

Cost	£80.00
Mark-up @ 25%	£20.00
Selling price	£100.00

The cost figure might be:

- total cost – the mark-up would be set to provide a profit per unit
- manufacturing cost – the mark-up would have to provide for non-manufacturing costs as well as profit
- marginal cost – the mark-up would have to contribute to fixed costs and profit.

An example of total cost-plus pricing:

Direct material cost	£40.00
Direct labour cost	£25.00
Direct expense	£15.00
Prime cost	£80.00
Indirect manufacturing cost	£20.00
Manufacturing cost	£100.00
Non-manufacturing overhead	£40.00
Total cost	£140.00
Mark-up, say 20% on cost	£28.00
Selling price	£168.00

Problems with this method are:

- The indirect manufacturing cost figure is based on estimates of expenditure and activity which may not reflect actual costs.
- The non-manufacturing overhead figure is even more of a guesstimate.
- How should the percentage mark-up be calculated?
- Will the product sell at £168?

Using the above figure of £100 manufacturing cost, the mark-up on this to give the same selling price would have to be much higher to provide for the non-manufacturing cost and profit. Here the percentage mark-up on manufacturing cost would be 68 per cent.

Cost-plus using marginal cost

Suppose in the example above the marginal cost was as follows:

Prime cost	£80.00
Variable manufacturing cost	£10 00
Variable non-manufacturing cost	£20.00
Marginal cost	£110.00

The mark-up on the marginal cost could be calculated to give a required contribution per unit, a target contribution/sales percentage or a target contribution per limiting factor.

Cost-plus using activity based costing

Some of the problems associated with total cost-plus may be avoided by using ABC cost information. Using ABC we might calculate the cost of the above product as follows:

Prime cost	£80.00
Indirects	£42.00
Total cost using ABC	£122.00

A mark-up could then be applied to the £122 to give a selling price structure which would be sufficient to pay for those overheads not allocated to products (because they are not controllable or activity driven) and to provide an adequate profit.

Establishing the target mark-up

One method of determining the target mark-up would be to use the master budget to establish the following:

Budgeted capital invested (I)	£1 000 000
Target return on capital (R)	25%
Therefore budgeted profit (P)	£250 000
Budgeted total annual costs (C)	£500 000
Budgeted sales (S)	£750 000
Target mark-up on costs	50%

The formula is:

$$\text{Mark-up \%} = I/C \times R$$
$$= 1\,000\,000/500\,000 \times 25\%$$
$$= 50\%$$

Using marginal costs   If the variable costs of the above firm were £250 000, the budgeted contribution would be sales – variable costs, or £500 000. If there was a limiting factor of 250 000 machine hours, the target contribution per limiting factor would be £500 000/250 000, or £2.00 per machine hour.

Therefore, if the marginal cost of a product was, say, £100 and it took 20 machine hours to make, the target contribution would be £40 and to achieve this the selling price would have to be £140.

Market pricing

The selling price is determined by considering prices charged for similar products. These prices denote what the market will bear and reflect competition.

The routine for market pricing is as follows:

- Establish the market price for similar products.
- Evaluate product differences.
- Price accordingly.

Market pricing does not obviate the need for cost information which indicates whether it is worth entering the market and enables the firm to rank products in order of profitability, perhaps by using contribution analysis.

Product differences need to be rated to arrive at the selling price. A scoring system should be devised so that each of the differences is compared with the competition and a final score arrived at. In the system in Table 7.1, 0 denotes no difference between the product and the competition.

Table 7.1 Evaluation of product differences

	Worse than				Better than		
	−3	−2	−1	0	+1	+2	+3
Design							
Performance							
Packaging							
Colour							
Appearance							
After-sales service							
Delivery							
Image/brand name							
Specification							
Payment terms							
Availability							

Price skimming

A higher price than normal is charged in the following circumstances:

- at the introduction of a new product for which there is not, as yet, any competition
- where there is a patent, for example the Xerox copier
- where the capital investment would be very high for a new entrant into the market.

Price penetration

Price penetration is usually introduced with a new product. The price is set at a lower level than normal to gain rapid acceptance in the market, which should be reasonably easy to enter.

The objective is to gain a large market share.

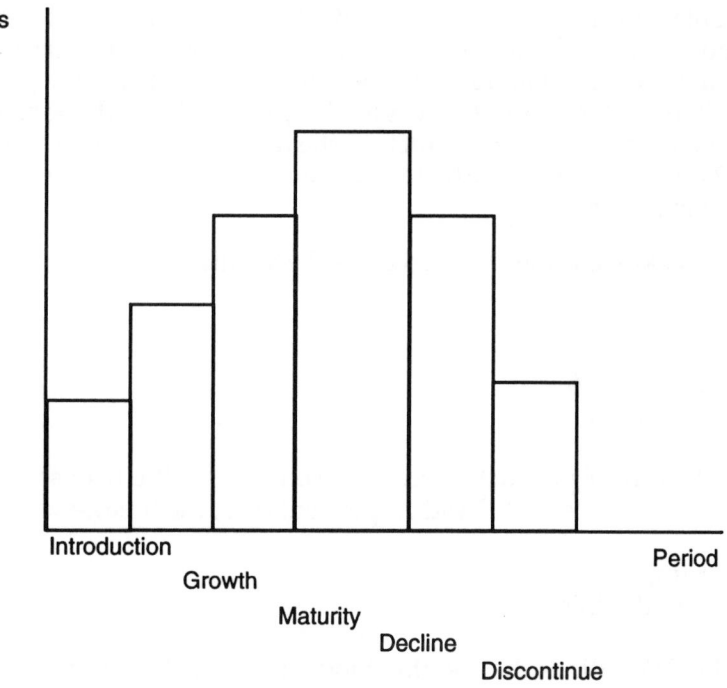

Figure 7.1   Product life cycle

Differential pricing

The price varies in different regions, with different order sizes, different customer groups and so on.

Product life cycle pricing

If a product is expected to go through the life cycle shown in Figure 7.1, the pricing policy could be adjusted to take account of the particular stage reached. At the outset a policy of price skimming or penetration pricing could be adopted, whilst at the growth stage the pricing policy should reflect the longer term as there would be considerable life in the product. At the maturity stage a policy to encourage short-term profit should be adopted. Finally, discounting should be introduced at the decline stage before the product is discontinued and a new product is introduced. The car industry adopts such a life cycle policy.

Loss leaders

These are products which are sold at a low selling price to attract customers who will then be encouraged to buy other products which are more profitable. The danger is that the budgeted mix of products is not achieved and too much of the loss leader is sold. This would increase the break-even point, lower the margin of safety and reduce the profit.

Table 7.2 shows how a loss leader, product C, might be sold together with two more profitable products. If the fixed costs of the firm in Table 7.2 were £2 million then the budgeted break-even would be calculated using the following formula:

break-even point = fixed costs/P/V ratio

that is:

£2m/45.2%
= £4.4 million

If the mix of products were reversed, that is, the firm sold only 5 per cent of A, 20 per cent of B and 75 per cent of C, the break-even would be

£2m/24.2%
= £8.3 million

The P/V ratio is the weighted average of the P/V ratios of the three products (see Table 7.3).

Table 7.2   Budgeted mix with loss leader

Product	Selling price £	Marginal cost £	Contribution £	P/V ratio %	Budgeted mix %
A	12	6	6	50	75
B	9	6	3	33.3	20
C	5	4	1	20	5
					100

Table 7.3   Weighted average P/V ratio

Product	Budget		Actual	
A	50% × 75%	=37.5%	50% × 5%	= 2.5%
B	33.3% × 20%	= 6.7%	33.3% × 20%	= 6.7%
C	20% × 5%	= 1.0%	20% × 75%	=15.0%
		45.2%		24.2%

Sensitivity analysis

Sensitivity analysis looks at the effect on the bottom line profit of changes to selling prices, variable costs and fixed costs (see Table 7.4). Much depends on the relative proportions of variable and fixed costs and on profit margins.

Table 7.4 Sensitivity analysis

	Orig. budget £	Volume up 10%	Price up 10%	Variables down 10%	Fixed down 10%
Sales	500 000	550 000	550 000	500 000	500 000
Variable costs	300 000	330 000	300 000	270 000	300 000
Gross profit	200 000	220 000	250 000	230 000	200 000
Fixed costs	100 000	100 000	100 000	100 000	90 000
Profit	100 000	120 000	150 000	130 000	110 000
% change		20	50	30	10

Note: A 10 per cent drop in the selling price would give rise to a 50 per cent drop in the profit.

Sensitivity analysis is best carried out using a spreadsheet. The technique is perhaps better known as 'what if' calculation.

Some pricing strategies

- In a price war, try to cut costs, both fixed and variable, to the bone.
- If you have high fixed costs, maintaining volume is all important. Offer quantity discounts and be sure to keep major customers contributing to this volume.
- Maintain margins on smaller accounts.
- If you have high variable costs, purchasing is of prime importance, as is the maintenance of profit margins.
- Identify your more profitable products. Drop lossmakers and low margin products. Consider the profitability, or lack of it, of small orders and small customers.
- Be careful with discounts. Do not discount on normal business. Discount for volume and for special deals. Remember the loss leader situation. Do not allow sales and marketing to discount without authorisation.
- Do not reward sales personnel on the basis of short-term sales rather than long-term profits.
- Price increases should be announced in good time. If others in the business are increasing prices then move with them. Little and often is better than one big price increase. Move some prices down. Get the customers used to price movements.
- When increasing prices, try to re-package the product. Look again at the list of product differences on pages 117–18.
- Stress product features – quality, availability, after-sales service – as alternatives to price.

8 Investment appraisal

This chapter is concerned with long-term investments in fixed assets, projects and investments in other companies. Techniques such as pay-back, accounting rate of return and discounted cash flow will be examined and the application of computerised spreadsheets will again be illustrated.

The investment of large sums of money in capital projects for an extended period of time is of great importance to the management of a business. A mistake in this area will have a much greater effect, and for much longer, than a mistake in the working capital area. Capital projects need to be appraised to see if they make sense financially.

Rate of return

One of the key ratios in determining financial strengths and weaknesses of a capital project is return on capital employed. The rate of return required by management will be determined by:

- the risk-free return available
- the cost of the firm's capital
- the riskiness of the investment
- the present rate of return.

Applications of investment appraisal

Investment appraisal should be carried out before

- purchasing a new machine or property
- making lease or buy decisions
- choosing between alternatives

- acquiring a company
- investing in research and development
- investing surplus funds
- making cost saving proposals on existing processes.

Cash flows

All the project appraisal methods use the concept of cash flow: cash is invested in a project and streams of cash flows will be generated in the future. Cash flow is used rather than profit because profit is subject to the judgements of depreciation, stock levels, accruals and provisions.

Cash inflows are assumed to arrive at the year end. Year 0 is when the cash outflow occurs. In a long-term construction project, for example, year 0 is when the first sod is cut.

Investment appraisal methods

Pay-back

This method calculates how long the future cash flows will take to pay back the initial investment. The faster the investment is returned the less the risk of losing it.

Many firms set a required pay-back period for a project to be acceptable. The problem, however, is that the cash inflows after the pay-back period has ended are ignored. For instance, a project could pay back the original investment in, say, three years and then cash flows cease. This, of course, would be less profitable than a project that pays back in four years but produces cash flows for 25 years.

Many companies use the method as an eliminator, subjecting those projects that pass the pay-back test to more stringent appraisal.

A variation of the method is to convert the future cash flows to their present value (see page 127), so recognising the time value of money. The discounted amounts must then pay back within a stipulated time period.

The following is an example of the pay-back method:

Initial investment in a machine: £120 000

Projected cash inflows:

	£
Year 1	30 000
Year 2	50 000
Year 3	80 000
Year 4	40 000
Year 5	10 000

Total	210 000

The pay-back period is $2\frac{1}{2}$ years because the future cash flows will pay back the £120 000 in that time span.

EXERCISE

The board of directors of HIJ Ltd have set a three year pay-back criterion for all capital investment. Two projects have been submitted to the capital investment committee and you are required to evaluate these.

1   Do both projects satisfy the board's criteria?
2   Which project would you recommend?

	Project 1	Project 2
Initial investment	80 000	160 000
Projected cash flows:		
Year 1	20 000	40 000
Year 2	40 000	50 000
Year 3	50 000	60 000
Year 4		100 000
Year 5		80 000
Year 6		70 000

ANSWER

Project 1 pays back the initial investment within the stipulated three years whilst project 2 does not. If the board are inflexible then project 2 would be rejected.

Project 2 cash inflows continue for far longer than project 1's and overall project 2 appears to have better long-term prospects.

Other factors to take into account would be:

● the relative amounts of the initial investment, that of project 2 being double that of project 1
● the accuracy of the projections of future cash flow; the further one projects into the future, the less accurate the projections will become.

With advanced manufacturing techniques (AMT) requiring much larger capital outlays and much longer cash inflows, the traditional pay-back method may be inappropriate. The Japanese tend to look at a much longer pay-back period than is the case in the West.

Accounting rate of return

This method compares the average annual return with the average capital investment and calculates the average rate of return. This rate of return can then be compared with the rate required by management. It could also be used to compare competing projects.

Table 8.1   Accounting rate of return

	Project 1	Project 2
Cash inflows	£110 000	£400 000
Cash outflow	£80 000	£160 000
Surplus	£30 000	£240 000
Surplus p.a.	£10 000	£40 000
Average investment	£40 000	£80 000
Average return on investment (ROI)	25%	50%

The problems with this method are:

- cash inflows do not come in at the same rate each year
- it does not recognise the 'time value' of money – the fact that a pound in your pocket now is better than a pound to be received in a year's time.

The example in Table 8.1 uses the figures from the exercise on page 125. This confirms the prediction that project 2 appeared to have better prospects.

The average investment is 50 per cent of the initial outlay, the assumption being that the cash inflows pay back the investment in equal instalments. The average investment would therefore be the amount outstanding halfway through the project life, that is, 50 per cent of the original investment.

EXERCISE

Calculate the accounting rate of return generated by the following project.

Initial investment year 0	£108 000

Cash inflows:

Year 1	£24 000
Year 2	£56 000
Year 3	£124 000
Year 4	£106 000
Year 5	£30 000

ANSWER

Cash flows generated	£340 000
Original investment	£108 000
Surplus	£232 000
Average surplus p.a.	£46 000
Average investment	£54 000
Average ROI	85.9%

Discounted cash flow

The previous methods of investment appraisal do not recognise the 'time value' of money.

A pound now is more valuable than a pound in a year's time because the pound now can be invested to earn interest and in a year's time would have grown to, say, £1.05 (if the interest rate was 5 per cent). A pound now can buy goods that will probably cost more in a year's time and a pound now is certain whilst the promise of a pound in the future may not materialise.

EXERCISE

If you could invest £1000 for five years at 10 per cent p.a. compound, that is, the interest is re-invested, what would it grow to by the end of the fifth year?

ANSWER

The £1000, which is known as the **present value** (PV), invested at 10 per cent p.a. for five years will grow as follows:

Year	Future value £
1	1100
2	1210
3	1331
4	1464
5	1661

The formula for calculating the **future value** (FV) of a sum of money (PV) is:

$$FV = PV \times (1+i)^n$$

where i = interest rate
n = the number of years the sum is invested.

The FV of £1000 invested at 12 per cent p.a. for four years would therefore be:

$$FV = 1000 \times (1+.12)^4$$
$$= 1573.52$$

Discounting calculates the PV of a sum of money to be received in the future. The formula is:

$$PV = FV/(1+i)^n$$

Table 8.2   Discount factors for £1 to be received in N years at rate R%

Rate year 1	2	3	4	5	6	7	8	9	10
1 0.990	0.980	0.971	0.962	0.952	0.943	0.935	0.926	0.917	0.909
2 0.980	0.961	0.943	0.925	0.907	0.890	0.873	0.857	0.842	0.826
3 0.971	0.942	0.915	0.889	0.864	0.840	0.816	0.794	0.772	0.751
4 0.961	0.924	0.888	0.855	0.823	0.792	0.763	0.735	0.708	0.683
5 0.951	0.906	0.863	0.822	0.784	0.747	0.713	0.681	0.650	0.621
6 0.942	0.888	0.837	0.790	0.746	0.705	0.666	0.630	0.596	0.564
7 0.933	0.871	0.813	0.760	0.711	0.665	0.623	0.583	0.547	0.513
8 0.923	0.853	0.789	0.731	0.677	0.627	0.582	0.540	0.502	0.467
9 0.914	0.837	0.766	0.703	0.645	0.592	0.544	0.500	0.460	0.424
10 0.905	0.820	0.744	0.676	0.614	0.558	0.508	0.463	0.422	0.386
11 0.896	0.804	0.722	0.650	0.585	0.527	0.475	0.429	0.388	0.350
12 0.887	0.788	0.701	0.625	0.557	0.497	0.444	0.397	0.356	0.319
13 0.879	0.773	0.681	0.601	0.530	0.469	0.415	0.368	0.326	0.290
14 0.870	0.758	0.661	0.577	0.505	0.442	0.388	0.340	0.299	0.263
15 0.861	0.743	0.642	0.555	0.481	0.471	0.362	0.315	0.275	0.239
16 0.853	0.728	0.623	0.534	0.458	0.394	0.339	0.292	0.252	0.218
17 0.844	0.714	0.605	0.513	0.436	0.371	0.317	0.270	0.231	0.198
18 0.836	0.700	0.587	0.494	0.416	0.350	0.296	0.250	0.212	0.180
19 0.828	0.686	0.570	0.475	0.396	0.331	0.277	0.232	0.194	0.164
20 0.820	0.673	0.554	0.456	0.377	0.312	0.258	0.215	0.178	0.149

Rate year 11	12	13	14	15	16	17	18	19	20
1 0.901	0.893	0.885	0.877	0.870	0.862	0.855	0.847	0.840	0.833
2 0.812	0.797	0.783	0.769	0.756	0.743	0.731	0.718	0.706	0.694
3 0.731	0.712	0.693	0.675	0.658	0.641	0.624	0.609	0.593	0.579
4 0.659	0.636	0.613	0.592	0.572	0.552	0.534	0.516	0.499	0.482
5 0.593	0.567	0.543	0.519	0.497	0.476	0.456	0.437	0.419	0.402
6 0.535	0.507	0.480	0.519	0.432	0.410	0.390	0.370	0.352	0.335
7 0.482	0.452	0.425	0.400	0.376	0.354	0.333	0.314	0.296	0.279
8 0.434	0.404	0.376	0.351	0.327	0.305	0.285	0.266	0.249	0.233
9 0.391	0.361	0.333	0.308	0.284	0.263	0.243	0.225	0.209	0.194
10 0.352	0.322	0.295	0.270	0.247	0.227	0.208	0.191	0.176	0.162
11 0.317	0.287	0.261	0.237	0.215	0.195	0.178	0.162	0.148	0.135
12 0.286	0.257	0.231	0.208	0.187	0.168	0.152	0.137	0.124	0.112
13 0.258	0.229	0.204	0.182	0.163	0.145	0.130	0.116	0.104	0.093
14 0.232	0.205	0.181	0.160	0.141	0.125	0.111	0.099	0.088	0.078
15 0.209	0.183	0.160	0.140	0.123	0.108	0.095	0.084	0.074	0.065
16 0.188	0.163	0.141	0.123	0.107	0.093	0.081	0.071	0.062	0.054
17 0.170	0.146	0.125	0.108	0.093	0.080	0.069	0.060	0.052	0.045
18 0.153	0.130	0.111	0.095	0.081	0.069	0.059	0.051	0.044	0.038
19 0.138	0.116	0.098	0.083	0.070	0.060	0.051	0.043	0.037	0.031
20 0.124	0.104	0.087	0.073	0.061	0.051	0.043	0.037	0.031	0.026

Therefore if £1000 was to be received at the end of year 4 with a discount rate of 10 per cent, its present value would be:

$$PV = 1000/(1+.1)^4$$
$$= 1000/1.4641$$
$$= 683$$

Conversely, if £683 were invested at 10 per cent p.a. compound it would grow to £1000 in four years.

The factor $1/(1+i)^n$ can be obtained from tables (see Table 8.2) or can be calculated using a calculator or computer.

Tables 8.3 and 8.4 use the spreadsheet to calculate the present values of the future cash flows for projects 1 and 2.

The discount rate has been taken as 20 per cent and the factors for each year have been computed. Multiplying the future cash flows by the corresponding factor gives the present value of those cash flows.

The present value of the initial investment is that investment – a negative cash outflow – and this is added to the positive future cash inflows to give the net present value (NPV). For project 1 the NPV is –6.620K and for project 2 +46.596K. What this means is that project 1 does not give a return of 20 per cent p.a. but something less. If the NPV had been zero then the

Table 8.3 Discounted cash flow – project 1

Discount rate: 20%			Initial investment: £80 000	
Years	$(1+i)^n$	$1/(1+i)^n$	Cash flows FV (£ 000s)	Cash flow PV (£000s)
0	1.000	1	–80	–80.000
1	1.200	0.833	20	16.667
2	1.440	0.694	40	27.778
3	1.728	0.579	50	28.935
4	2.074	0.482		0.000
5	2.488	0.402		0.000
6	2.986	0.335		0.000
7	3.583	0.279		0.000
8	4.300	0.233		0.000
9	5.160	0.194		0.000
10	6.192	0.162		0.000
Net present value				–6.620

Table 8.4 Discounted cash flow – project 2

Discount rate: 20%			Initial investment: £160 000	
Years	$(1+i)^n$	$1/(1+i)^n$	Cash flows FV (£ 000s)	Cash flow PV (£000s)
0	1.000	1	–160	–160.000
1	1.200	0.833	40	33.333
2	1.440	0.694	50	34.722
3	1.728	0.579	60	34.722
4	2.074	0.482	100	48.225
5	2.488	0.402	80	32.150
6	2.986	0.335	70	23.443
7	3.583	0.279		0.000
8	4.300	0.233		0.000
9	5.160	0.194		0.000
10	6.192	0.162		0.000
Net present value				46.596

project would have given us exactly 20 per cent p.a. (and our money back). Project 2 gives us more than 20 per cent p.a. and our original investment back. Project 2 is therefore acceptable whilst project 1 is not.

Projects can be ranked in order of profitability using the profitability index:

$$\frac{\text{total PV of future cash flows}}{\text{initial investment}}$$

For a project to be acceptable this must be more than 1. For project 2 the figure is

$$\frac{206.6}{160} = 1.29$$

Internal rate of return

Another way of using discounted cash flow (DCF) is to calculate what rate of discount produces a net present value (NPV) of zero. This is known as the **internal rate of return** (IRR).

Looking again at projects 1 and 2, the rate of discount that produces a zero NPV is 15.3 per cent for project 1 and 29.7 per cent for project 2 (Tables 8.5 and 8.6). This means that project 1 will give 15.3 per cent p.a. and the original investment back whilst project 2 gives 29.7 per cent and the investment returned. It can be useful to rank projects in order of their IRRs.

Tables 8.7 and 8.8 have been used to produce Figure 8.1 and show the NPV at different discount rates.

At a discount rate of 18% the NPV is positive and the project is acceptable; the discount rate giving a NPV of zero is 21.8%, the internal rate of return (IRR). The pay-back is about 2 years and 5 months.

Table 8.5   Using discounted cash flow to calculate internal rate of return – project 1

Discount rate: 15.3%			Initial investment: £80 000	
Years	$(1+i)^n$	$1/(1+i)^n$	Cash flows FV (£000s)	Cash flow PV (£000s)
0	1.000	1	−80	−80.000
1	1.153	0.867	20	17.346
2	1.329	0.752	40	30.089
3	1.533	0.652	50	32.620
4	1.767	0.566		0.000
5	2.038	0.491		0.000
6	2.350	0.426		0.000
7	2.709	0.369		0.000
8	3.123	0.320		0.000
9	3.601	0.278		0.000
10	4.152	0.241		0.000
Net present value				0.054

Table 8.6   Using discounted cash flow to calculate internal rate of return – project 2

Discount rate: 29.7%			Initial investment: £160 000	
Years	$(1+i)^n$	$1/(1+i)^n$	Cash flows FV (£000s)	Cash flow PV (£000s)
0	1.000	1	−160	−160.000
1	1.297	0.771	40	30.840
2	1.682	0.594	50	29.723
3	2.182	0.458	60	27.500
4	2.830	0.353	100	35.338
5	3.670	0.272	80	21.797
6	4.760	0.210	70	14.705
7	6.174	0.162		0.000
8	8.008	0.125		0.000
9	10.386	0.096		0.000
10	13.471	0.074		0.000
Net present value				−0.098

Table 8.7   Evaluating an investment of £140 000 using a discount rate of 18 per cent

Discount rate: 18%			Initial investment: (£000s) 140	
Years	$(1+i)^n$	$1/(1+i)^n$	Cash flows FV	Cash flow PV
0	1.000	1	−140	−140.000
1	1.180	0.847	60	50.847
2	1.392	0.718	60	43.091
3	1.643	0.609	50	30.432
4	1.939	0.516	50	25.789
5	2.288	0.437		0.000
6	2.700	0.370		0.000
7	3.185	0.314		0.000
8	3.759	0.266		0.000
9	4.435	0.225		0.000
10	5.234	0.191		0.000
Net present value				10.160

Table 8.8   Evaluating an investment of £140 000 using a discount rate of 21.8 per cent

Discount rate: 21.8%			Initial investment: (£000s) 140	
Years	$(1+i)^n$	$1/(1+i)^n$	Cash flows FV	Cash flow PV
0	1.000	1	−140	−140.000
1	1.218	0.821	60	49.261
2	1.484	0.674	60	40.444
3	1.807	0.553	50	27.671
4	2.201	0.454	50	22.719
5	2.681	0.373		0.000
6	3.265	0.306		0.000
7	3.977	0.251		0.000
8	4.844	0.206		0.000
9	5.900	0.170		0.000
10	7.186	0.139		0.000
Net present value				0.095

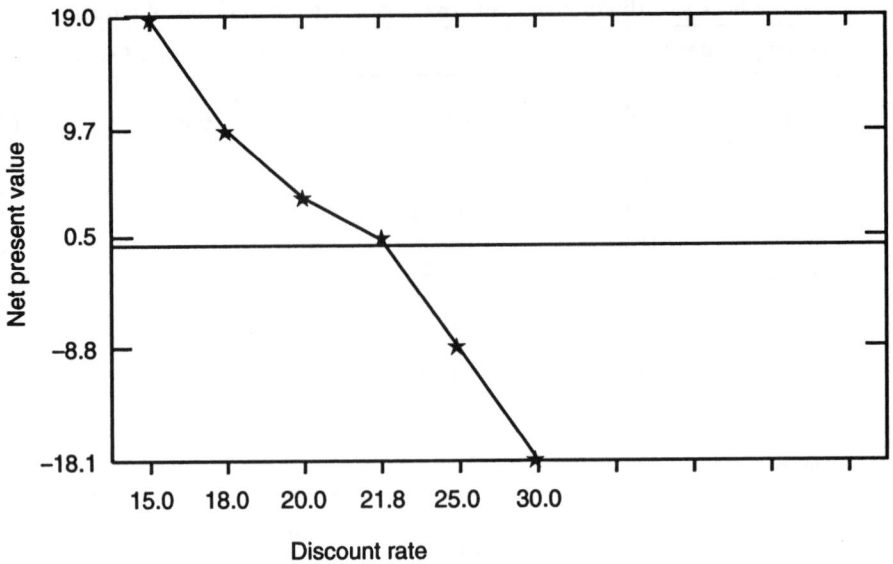

Figure 8.1   Discounted cash flow

Sensitivity analysis

This technique tests the effects of changes in the various assumptions in the DCF calculations on the final outcome. If a large percentage change to an assumption has a small percentage change on the outcome then the project is said to be 'robust'. A small percentage change on an assumption giving a large percentage change on the outcome is an example of a 'sensitive' project.

Probability analysis

Closely allied to sensitivity analysis is probability analysis where management require projects to be subjected to probability factors giving the most likely, the best and the worst likely outcomes.

Both these techniques come under the heading of 'what if?' analysis and are best performed using a computer.

Summary

Whatever methods management apply in capital project appraisal, of most importance is the accuracy of the projections of future cash flow. If these are inaccurate then everything is inaccurate.

9 Management decision making using financial data

In business, managers have to plan, control and make decisions and, in making decisions that involve money, the manager will rely on the relevant data being presented by the finance department.

The financial presentation should detail the likely financial implications of alternative courses of action and may recommend one course of action over another. Any assumptions and estimates should be clearly stated. The decision-making function is still in the hands of management and not finance, but management must have timely, accurate and relevant information, and an understanding of what is meant by 'relevant' data.

Relevant data

Decisions have to be made whenever there are choices. The decision to do nothing is still a decision!

Decisions can be split into two basic types:

1 accept or reject decisions – only one opportunity exists to make the decision
2 ranking decisions – more than one opportunity exists but not all can be taken up because of limited resources or because the opportunities may be mutually exclusive.

When financial data is to be used in decision making it must be:

- relevant
- accurate
- timely
- related to the time period of the decision, that is, the future.

Relevant costs

Some costs are relevant to the decision being made whereas others – irrelevant costs – can be ignored in decision making. Examples of relevant costs are:

- future marginal cost (see pp. 38–43).
- differential cost. This is defined as the additional cost of one course of action over another and is also known as incremental cost. This concept is often used when deciding between competing projects. Costs common to competing projects can be ignored in decision making.
- opportunity cost. This is defined as the contribution lost by choosing one alternative rather than another.

  For example, in considering the production of a special component which is currently bought in, the choice has to be made whether surplus space is rented out for £5000 p.a. or the space is used by the organisation itself to make the component.

  The decision to make the component gives rise to an opportunity cost of £5000 – the lost rental income. This should be taken into account when deciding whether to make or buy.

  Using materials to manufacture the component that originally cost £10 000 but have a scrap value of £3000 would mean an opportunity cost of £3000 – the lost contribution. This is a relevant cost. The £10 000 would be a sunk cost and therefore irrelevant.

Different costs for different purposes

Management should understand that costs and revenues thrown up by the financial accounting system need to be treated with caution in decision making. Opportunity costs are, of course, not costs at all. They are lost profits (contributions) that will not form part of the financial accounts.

Further examples of management accounting costs not forming part of the financial accounts are **notional costs**, such as notional interest on capital invested in a department (even if the firm has no borrowings).

In financial accounting there are rules laid down by the accounting profession and by the Inland Revenue as to the methods to be used for stock valuations. These should in no way restrict the use of other methods which would be more appropriate in management accounting.

The oil refining industry provides an example of the use of different costs for different purposes. Oil refining is a continuous process and by-products are often produced. The revenues from the by-products are often treated as a reduction in the cost of the process which produced the main product or joint products. How the cost of the process is split over the joint products is an interesting decision. The by-products can perhaps be further processed after the split-off point (where products become separately identified). The decision whether to sell the by-product as it is or to subject it to further processing will be based on a comparison between its net realisable value now and its net realisable value after further processing less further processing costs.

EXERCISE

A management training company has spent £1500 on printing 5000 brochures and mailing them to potential customers. It has booked a conference room at a hotel which costs £250 for the day. Meals and refreshments will be provided at £12 per delegate. There is a cancellation fee of 25 per cent of the room rate. A speaker has agreed to lecture on the day for a fee of £400. If the event is cancelled then no fee is payable. Brochures and handouts for the day will cost the company £3 per delegate. Delegates pay £200 for the day. One week before the course there are four bookings. Should the course be cancelled?

ANSWER

The course organisers need to split the costs into those that have already been incurred, the **sunk costs** and the future marginal costs, as follows:

Sunk costs		
Printing and mailing		£1500
Future marginal costs		
Room hire	£250	
Delegate rate	£48	
Speaker	£400	
Brochures	£12	
		£710
Fees from delegates		£800
Net benefit		£90

The course should be run because there will be a contribution of £90 towards the sunk cost of £1500. The overall loss on the event will be £1410. If the course was not run the sunk cost would increase by £62.50, the cancellation fee.

Another consideration if the course was cancelled is the loss of goodwill. It is unlikely the four delegates would book on to a further course. Running the course with four delegates would be a good PR exercise (they would also benefit from individual attention).

EXERCISE

PPK Ltd has surplus production space which it could rent to a neighbouring company for £10 000 p.a.

The sales manager wants to take on a special order with a selling price of £30 000. The material to be used originally cost £12 000 but has a market value of £3000. Direct labour to be employed just for this job would cost £15 000. Variable overheads, power, freight and so on would amount to £8000.

Fixed costs are recovered on all jobs by applying a recovery rate of £1 of fixed cost per £1 of direct labour.

Should the job be carried out?

ANSWER

	Relevant £	Irrelevant £	
Material	3 000		Opportunity cost
		12 000	Sunk cost
Labour	15 000		Future marginal
Variable indirects	8 000		Future marginal
Fixed costs recovered		15 000	Incurred anyway
Rental income foregone	10 000		Opportunity cost
Total	36 000		
Revenue	30 000		
Cost	6 000		

As the cost is £6000 more than the benefit the job should be turned down.

EXERCISE

SK Motors is about to close its Brighton works where it made sports cars. A former customer has asked whether he could order one last car before the factory is dismantled.

1   There are sufficient materials for the bodywork in stock which originally cost £3000 but have a disposal value of £950.
2   There are sufficient stocks of engine parts which originally cost £2200. These were to be transported to a Bristol factory at a cost of £300. Bristol would currently expect to pay £2000 for these parts.
3   Direct labour and variable overheads are estimated to be £2800.
4   A spare supervisor would be sent from Bristol for the week needed to make the car. His normal wage is £300 and his travelling and hotel bill would amount to £400.
5   Fixed costs have been recovered at the rate of £2 per £1 of direct costs.

Would you accept an offer of £7000 for the special order?

ANSWER

		Relevant £	Irrelevant £	
1	Material	950		Opportunity cost
			3000	Sunk cost
2	Parts	1700		Net opportunity
			2200	Sunk cost
3	Labour etc.	2800		Future marginals
4	Supervisor	400		Future marginals
			300	Fixed
5	Fixed costs recovered			Incurred anyway
		5850		
	Selling price	7000		
	Net benefit	1150		

Therefore, on purely financial grounds, the order should be accepted.

Make or buy decisions

Management may have to decide whether to buy in a component from an outside third party or to continue manufacture of the product itself.

In make or buy decisions the relevant costs are those avoided if a particular course of action is not taken. The avoidable cost of purchasing if the company decides to make is the price quoted by the supplier. The avoidable cost of making if the company decides to buy would be the future marginal costs such as direct materials, direct labour and variable overheads as well as such opportunity costs as sale of stock at current value or rental income.

In addition, certain non-financial factors will need to be considered such as:

- Will quality be maintained?
- Will delivery dates be met?
- Will there be unexpected price rises?
- What will be done with the space and personnel now no longer needed to make this product?
- Will the plant and machinery used now be used to make something else?

Product selection

Our earlier investigation into marginal costing (see pages 38–43) suggested a method of deciding which products to make in preference to others. Much depended on whether there was a key or limiting factor, in which case the contribution per limiting factor would be the deciding figure.

Activity based costing (ABC) can also be used in this area. This generates more accurate product cost information than absorption costing, particularly when overheads form a high percentage of total cost.

Such information could form the basis of activity based management (ABM) where decisions have to be made concerning which products to produce in priority over others or which distribution channels to use. For example, decisions as to whether to source supply from UK manufacturers or from overseas can be made using ABC, and decisions relating to minimum order values may be aided by an up to date activity based cost for producing an invoice.

Another approach is **throughput accounting** (TA) which is similar to the idea of maximising the contribution per limiting factor. The key measure, the throughput, is defined as sales less material costs. The assumption of TA is that all costs except materials are fixed in relation to changes in throughput in the short term.

The profitability of products is determined by how quickly they generate contribution (the throughput). The method depends on the identification and elimination (if possible) of bottlenecks and constraints.

10 Conclusion

This book has been written from a managerial viewpoint rather than as a textbook. Much of what is known as Finance and Management Accounts would be much easier to understand if it was not obscured by the use of jargon. Indeed, the majority of the techniques described here are quite easy to understand, based as they are on logic.

Business is about mixing people and money together and, of the two, people are more important. It is people who make things happen, not money.

Managers, although often highly skilled in their own particular area of expertise, are often at a loss when presented with financial data. Nevertheless, the language of business is money and managers, to be really effective, must learn this language. Hopefully, this book will have removed much of the mystique attached to management accounts.

The advent of the spreadsheet and accounting software has lead to an explosion of information in both numeric and graphical form, often in glorious technicolour. Such information is useless unless it is understood by the non-financial manager and then used to control the business. Many managers have remarked that when they were presented with the results in the form of ratios all the pieces seemed to fit together and the 'big picture' became clear. The selection of appropriate ratios and the keeping of some form of financial scorecard will provide the basis for more effective control of the business.

In summary, the key points to remember when handling financial information are as follows:

- If you receive financial information you do not understand or cannot use, tell your accountant.
- If you are inundated with jargon you do not understand, ask for definitions.
- If there is information you need but are not receiving, tell your

139

accountant.

- If there is information you are receiving that you do not need, tell your accountant.
- Be certain about the unit cost of your products. Question the methods of allocating overheads to products.
- Budgets should be believable, achievable and should have involved the managers in their preparation.
- Financial data should arrive in the right form, at the right time and be accurate enough for management action.
- Remember the following:

'Sales are vanity, profits are sanity.'
'Cash is reality.'

Index

MTA

Tony Skone is principal of MTA, Management & Training Associates.

MTA's unique approach takes anyone with little or no financial background to an UNDERSTANDING of the key concepts of finance, accounts and budgets.

FINAL ANALYSIS

An important element of MTA's training sessions is the use of our specially-developed computer software applications enabling clients to present and analyse their financial data and those of their customers, suppliers and competitors. Our best selling 'spreadsheet work-alike' programme is **FINAL ANALYSIS.**

Here are some of the things it can do for you:

- generate cash flow and added value statements
- calculate key management ratios
- evaluate Z-scores, financial strength and cash conversion periods
- display these analyses in the form of data tables or in startling colour-graphics
- provide instant on-line context-sensitive help; the Help Screens explain the statements you are reading, define the ratios, or explain how to make best use of the many menu-driven program functions.

The normal commercial price of **FINAL ANALYSIS** is £199.95 plus VAT, but we are making a special offer to readers of this book. You can obtain a full working copy for only £169.95 plus VAT, inclusive of posting and package, by completing the application form below.

To: Management & Training Associates, PO Box 658, Harrow, Middlesex HA3 6DX
    Tel: 081 954 5701   Fax: 081 954 4337

Please send me _____ copy/copies of **FINAL ANALYSIS** at your special offer price of £169.95 plus VAT*

My cheque for £_____ is enclosed.

*Special Licence Prices are available for schools and other educational establishments. Please contact MTA for details.

Please send me further information on:

MTA Training Courses	☐
FINAL ANALYSIS	☐
Business Simulations	☐
Other Software	☐

Name . . . .

Position . . . .

Company . . . .

Address . . . .

. . . .

. . . . Post Code: . . . .

Tel . . . . Fax . . . .

Signature . . . . Date . . . .

Beyond the Bottom Line
Advanced Financial Management in Business

Alan Warner

A Gower Novel

In this fascinating sequel to *The Bottom Line* Phil Moorley finds himself president of a large US food manufacturer, and facing a takeover bid from Universal, his previous employer. He finds that the financial knowledge acquired in *The Bottom Line* is not enough to cope with this new challenge. As before, he turns for help to blonde, beautiful management consultant Christine Goodhart. The takeover bid is resolved and, in the course of it, the reader learns about: • evaluating an acquisition • price/earnings ratio and market capitalization • treatment of goodwill • asset valuations, including brands • dividend yield and dividend cover • the factors affecting share price.

Moorley offers Christine the job as his VP Finance, with consequences which do more for his company than for his marriage. The second half of the book describes how Phil and Christine work together to develop improved management accounting information systems to support their strategic decision-making. The subjects covered include: • principles of financial measurement • replacement cost accounting • limiting factor analysis • price/volume sensitivities • ratios for competitor analysis • Pareto analysis of product/customer profiles • strategic profitability evaluations • post audit of investment appraisals • direct product profitability techniques.

Readers will find that they are able to consolidate the knowledge gained from *The Bottom Line* and be introduced to some advanced but practical concepts of finance rarely dealt with in conventional textbooks.

1993   231 pages   0 566 07479 6

A Gower Paperback

The Bottom Line
Practical Financial Management in Business

Alan Warner

A Gower Novel

In this remarkable book Alan Warner uses the power of romantic fiction to explain the key concepts of business finance. By creating a believable set of characters and a compelling story he has provided an easy and enjoyable way to understand balance sheets, budgeting, marginal costing, investment appraisal, profit maximization, performance measurement and other modern accounting techniques.

The story concerns Phil Moorley, Sales and Marketing Director of Lawrence & Sons, and his relationship with Christine Goodhart, the management accountant imposed on the company by its conglomerate owners. Moorley's big professional weakness is his lack of financial knowledge, but with Chris' help he begins to learn – and the reader learns with him. In the process his feelings for Chris grow stronger – but will she ever be willing to offer him more than friendship and tutorials? After a number of crises, Moorley begins to prepare himself for a more ambitious role. Then fate steps in, and both his business and personal life take a swift new turn.

The Bottom Line is as far from a conventional textbook as can be imagined. Its readability and its business setting combine to make it the best possible introduction to business finance for the non-accountant.

1993   256 pages   0 566 07480 X

A Gower Paperback

The Business Plan – Approved!

G Nigel Cohen

The Business Plan - Approved! is a comprehensive guide to creating an impressive and achievable business plan to win the approval of your bank manager and investors. It will help you to evaluate the business from the viewpoints of sales, costs, and cash and assimilate the information into a clearly defined business strategy. Written in a clear, down-to-earth style, with no technical jargon, it encourages you to see your business plan as a potential investor in the company would, answering some basic but crucial questions along the way:

- What is a business plan and why do we need one?
- How do we go about creating a successful business plan?
- What do banks and investors look for?

All aspects of the business plan are dealt with, from initial planning in order to decide which direction the business should follow, through to presenting the plan in a professional and persuasive document. Guidance is also provided on how to set the plan out in the style that bankers and investors expect to see.

Written by accountants with many years' experience of getting plans approved and vetting them for banks and investors, uniquely this book also includes the expert opinions of investors and lawyers themselves describing what makes them accept or reject a business plan. Two real life examples are provided as models and to focus the reader on common pitfalls.

The practical, no-nonsense guidance of *The Business Plan – Approved!* will be welcomed by anyone planning to grow a business, start up on their own, or, as a manager, justify their budget for the coming year.

1994   192 pages   0 566 07453 2

A Gower Paperback

The Goal
Beating the Competition
Second Edition

Eliyahu M Goldratt and Jeff Cox

Written in a fast-paced thriller style, *The Goal* is the gripping novel which is transforming management thinking throughout the Western world.

Alex Rogo is a harried plant manager working ever more desperately to try to improve performance. His factory is rapidly heading for disaster. So is his marriage. He has ninety days to save his plant – or it will be closed by corporate HQ, with hundreds of job losses. It takes a chance meeting with a colleague from student days – Jonah – to help him break out of conventional ways of thinking to see what needs to be done.

The story of Alex's fight to save his plant is more than compulsive reading. It contains a serious message for all managers in industry and explains the ideas which underlie the Theory of Constraints (TOC) developed by Eli Goldratt – the author described by Fortune as 'a guru to industry' and by Businessweek as a 'genius'.

As a result of the phenomenal and continuing success of *The Goal*, there has been growing demand for a follow-up. Eliyahu Goldratt has now written ten further chapters which continues the story of Alex Rogo as he makes the transition from Plant Manager to Divisional Manager. Having achieved the turnround of his plant, Alex now attempts to apply all that Jonah has taught him, not to crisis management, but to ongoing improvement.

These new chapters reinforce the thinking process utilised in the first edition of *The Goal* and apply them to a wider management context with the aim of stimulating readers into using the technique in their own environment.

1993   352 pages   0 566 07418 4

A Gower Paperback

The Meaning of
Company Accounts
Fifth Edition

Walter Reid and D R Myddelton

The Meaning of Company Accounts first appeared in 1971 and quickly achieved recognition among managers, financial and non-financial alike. Its "workbook" approach stems from the need for a treatment of financial accounting practice which readers at differing levels of knowledge can tailor individually to their learning requirements. The authors, both of them distinguished teachers of finance and accounting, adopt programmed learning techniques within a firmly structured text in order to provide for a wide variety of readers' needs. At controlled points the reader is invited to work through examples and write into the workbook his or her solutions to problems. These active responses both reinforce what has been learned and extend the reader's experience and skill in using, preparing and interpreting company accounts.

For this fifth edition, the authors have revised their text to reflect recent developments, including new accounting standards and changes in company law. They have added material on brands, and an appendix of photocopiable formats covering financial ratios, segment analysis and cash/funds flow.

Contents
The background and structure of company accounts • Analysing company accounts • Recording business transactions • Measuring profit or loss • Fixed assets and depreciation • Cash flow statements • Company taxation • Capital structure • Group accounts • International accounting • Inflation accounting • Interpreting company accounts • Appendices • Solutions • Index.

1992   376 pages   0 566 07350 1

A Gower Paperback

Understanding BS5750
And Other Quality Systems

Tony Brown

More and more companies are considering adopting BS5750 (ISO9000) as they realise that failure to gain registration to BS5750 could mean the loss of existing customers and difficulty in securing new ones. This imperative exists regardless of the size of the firm or the type of industry. *Understanding BS5750* is written in plain language and is aimed at those with little or no knowledge of the subject. It is the most comprehensive book of its kind available and gives objective comment and advice on all the key aspects such as:

What is it? Why do you need it? Can you ignore it? What are the benefits and problems? What time scales are involved? What are the costs? What are the methods of gaining registration? How do you retain registration? What is a certification body? Are they all the same?

The book also provides a comprehensive directory of hundreds of names giving full information on: • Who can provide practical assistance• What subsidies are available • Details of all the UK certification bodies• Further reading • Glossary of terms.

Sections have been compiled examining the subject from the viewpoint of manufacturers, service organisations, the public sector and the professions. Other quality standards are also dealt with in considerable detail, including TQM, BS7750 and Tickit. The book is ideal for anyone in business requiring one comprehensive introduction to quality systems.

Contents

Introduction • General background to BS5750 • Quality standards • More detailed information on BS5750 • The changing nature of the quality market place • Industry and sector relevance • What to do next • Costs, timescales and other concerns • Certification bodies, background details, addresses and costs • Advantages/benefits and disadvantages to BS5750 • The fairly technical section • Other quality systems • Glossary of terms.

1993   176 pages   0 566 07455 9

A Gower Paperback

What Maastricht Means for Business

Opportunities and regulations in the EC Internal Market

Brian Rothery

A businessman's guide to the opportunities presented by the Maastricht Agreement, together with information on the implications of the resulting legislation for anyone managing a company in Europe, or trading with the European Community.

Contents

1993	272 pages	0 566 07431 1

A Gower Paperback